CW01305180

'Dishing th

Recollections of a TV Make-up Artist
A look behind the scenes at what really goes on.
Pictures and Stories of many major Drama Productions.
BBC & ATV
Including:
All Creatures Great & Small
Boys from the Black Stuff &
Peak Practice

Maggie Thomas

Authors On Line

Visit us online at www.authorsonline.co.uk

An Authors OnLine Book

ISBN 978-07552-0453-3

Authors OnLine Ltd
19 The Cinques
Gamlingay, Sandy
Bedfordshire SG19 3NU
England

This book is also available in e-book format, details of which are available at www.authorsonline.co.uk

Foreword

My thanks to my dear friend Judy Coyle for her considerable encouragement and help with 'large lumps' of typing, and without whom I may never have got off the starting blocks.
And to my many lovely make-up assistants who have helped me along the way.
Thanks to Richard and everyone at Authors On Line.
And lastly to my Guardian Angel who has always been there when things seemed impossible.

Contents

In The Beginning

In my wildest dreams I could not have imagined what the future had in store for me.

I was born in 1935 and by the time I was 4 years old World War 2 was starting, so I didn't have a very conventional childhood. My sister and I were shipped off to Cheshire to one of my father's childless brothers and his wife so that we wouldn't have to spend every night down in the air raid shelter. At this time we lived in the flat above the family business and the council had commandeered the cellars underneath to be made into public shelters. They had cut a hole in the pavement and put a staircase down for access to the underground cellars; this meant that we weren't getting any sleep because everyone was talking and singing and generally trying to take their minds off the bombs flying overhead.

In the early part of the war a great deal of damage was done to the lower part of Broad Street, where we lived. Our shop was just far enough up the street to be saved from any damage, but at the time it seemed as though the whole of the city would be flattened. So that's why my sister and I were sent off to Tattenhall and a very quiet country life.

I had been born into a family from Lancashire. Grandpa Salisbury had come to Birmingham at the start of the 1920s to seek his fortune. His daughter (my mother) was the daughter of a man who as a boy had worked at the age of 10 in a cotton mill in Blackburn and then was allowed to go to school in the afternoon. There is some wonderful old film that had been discovered by workmen demolishing a building; it was restored and shows amazing scenes shot by Mitchell and Kenyon. They were famous for shooting moving film of the ordinary people out and about on their High Days and Holidays in the North of England in the late 1800s. They were the first filmed record of sporting events and Bank Holiday outings. They also captured little boys coming out of the factories; it is shocking to see that child labour was still around so recently.

I am sure that my grandfather was amongst those little rag-a-muffins.

I treasure the film that I was able to copy off the television to hand down to my grandchildren.

So, by 1935 things had begun to be very comfortable – until 1939, when the bombs started falling.

Grandpa Salisbury had come from Kendal in Cumbria, where he had learned his knowledge of pork products and was a master curer of York hams, which he supplied to hotels in London. Wanting to extend his scope, he decided he needed to move to the Midlands, where the Victorians were making the pavements of gold and he could capitalise on his expertise. He bought a shop in the most fashionable street that was the main access to the shopping centre and when he had started to become successful he bought three acres of land 15 miles out of the city and built his dream house. He was an austere man who had never wasted money, and so the house was a complete move away from his previous cautious ways. To outward appearances it was an extravagant, luxury house, with balconies and arched windows; and even a huge stained-glass window at the head of the highly polished staircase, which extended up two floors high. The floors were teratso throughout the ground floor, except the kitchen, which strangely had a parquet woodblock floor. The furnishings were from London and a vast sideboard with a wall-to-wall mirror filled the huge dining room. Unfortunately, central heating had not been included in the plans and in winter it was like an ice box and every room had to have a coal fire lit in it. So, all that glittered was not gold.

As a 5-year-old child, the place terrified me: everywhere was so huge and outside there were no street lights, just black darkness that filled the world. I only realise now, looking back, that even if I had lived in the city the streets would still have been dark as by now everyone had to put up blackout curtains and there were no street lights in case the bomber aircraft used them to find their way to our cities. So it was to here that my sister and I returned when it was considered safe, but even so I was glad to be back home.

My father, who was the eldest son of a farmer/butcher in Tattenhall, a village near to Chester, was sent to Birmingham to learn the art of curing and other processes related to pork. He met my mother and never returned to Tattenhall to take back the knowledge or his rightful position as eldest son.

He continued to be Grandpa's right-hand man for the rest of his life, but never really took over the full running of the business as Richard Salisbury lived until he was nearly 90 and continued to go to work every day. By that time my poor father had had enough; the "Old Boy" had worn him out and he retired to the seaside.

So, from a very undistinguished period at a very expensive private school (Margaret could do better) and a rather disrupted home life. Food and clothes rationing hadn't really allowed me much scope to form any style or understanding of sophistication as it had been pre-war and I was too young to remember the Roaring 20s. By the time I was 18, leaving school was something of a dilemma.

I didn't really have any great expectations, except a strong desire to get married and have my own family. I loved cooking, but it still wasn't fashionable to do as a career and my parents were modern enough to insist on some attempt at a job until Mr. Right came along. So it was decided that I should start Nursing. That was something socially acceptable, and so it was that I started at The Eye Hospital and, after 9 months of living like a nun, I plucked up enough courage to tell my mother that I couldn't stand another moment of it.

Fortunately, I had very liberal parents and they allowed me to return home and managed to get me an apprenticeship with a hairdresser. I very soon found this was just being a dogsbody to the "stylists" and I was not learning anything productive to do with any aspect of cutting, colouring or perming. What I did learn from the resident beautician was that her job was much more appealing. So I suggested to my mother that it would be a good move for me to go to London and train. After some wheedling and cajoling, it was agreed that I could go, and then some interviews were arranged at three of the possible schools that ran courses in Bond Street or Bayswater. I chose the Jean Reid School of Beauty Therapy at Queensway, Bayswater, and was overcome with excitement until my ever-patient parents said that I must live in a Youth Hostel at Marble Arch to help keep the cost down. However, I felt they had been so sympathetic to let me get this far that I must be sensible and co-operate. I was sure that in no time I would talk them into some better arrangement.

In spite of a year in London at a beauty therapy school, I returned to Birmingham physically still a fat schoolgirl at 19. I had not benefited from the sophisticated life that should have turned the duckling into a swan. I don't think that sharing a room with assorted females in a YMCA at Marble Arch greatly contributed to a metamorphosis and living on a shoestring didn't allow me to take in much in the way of culture – even the cinema was too expensive for many visits – but just walking around London was awesome to me and satisfied my soul at that tender age. The highlight of the week was a visit to the salad bar in the basement of the Cumberland Palace Hotel. It was a revolutionary concept at that time where one could eat as much of the 50 or so choices of salads as possible followed by a huge piece of gateau and coffee for 4/6p, and all this in the glittering surroundings of one of the top hotels in London.

Another of our cheap thrills consisted of 'tangling' with the prostitutes down Park Lane, where we used to stroll for a coffee when funds allowed. These strangely uncommon creatures would leer at us and hiss 'gerorf our pitch'.

We eventually found another hot-spot that we could sometimes afford: that was the 100 Club in Oxford Street, where the very thin George Melly let his vocal hair down in the wildest way I have ever encountered. Backed by Humph

Lyttelton, they were both sweating like race horses all evening. It was the most exciting thing of all.

When the year was up I was surprisingly ready to return to Birmingham. I felt mostly relief to be in safe surroundings amongst friends and family, and this outweighed any loss of the bright lights. Anyway, Birmingham was quite a wonderful place in 1953. It still had great style and a wonderful feeling that the war was really over and anything was possible. There was a Marshall and Snelgrove and Barrows and Patterson's Tea Rooms where 'ladies' went for lunch or tea and really dressed up with beautiful suits, hats and expensive matching shoes and handbags, and town was a very glamorous place with lots of busy, exciting people and places to go. So my return from London was just the start of the best part of my life. Getting the job at Greatorex was a great achievement, as it really was one of the top five salons in the city at that time. My shyness and fatness were masked by the illusion of being a beautician trained in London and I thought my heart would burst on the first day I started work.

In 1953 I returned from the London College of Beauty Therapy and took the position of Junior Therapist in a seemingly very luxurious salon. The lady who owned the salon was also the Head Beautician. It didn't take very long for me to realise that I was to be a below-stairs dogsbody, at everyone's beck and call – from sweeping up cut hair to going for the lunch rolls and sorting the laundry. Oh well, everyone starts somewhere. The rest of the staff were very aware of their positions in the pecking order and made no bones about using the latest arrival as a skivvy. I was still young enough to feel grateful for a position in such a prestigious salon and I put my best foot forward in the hope of gaining approval by always being ready and willing, so that I might eventually be rewarded with more responsible tasks. After six months I had made a lot of friends and was having a lot of fun out of work hours.

I will say at this point that I had always been a misfit at school and in general I always felt different to all my associates, and now that I am older I think it was something to do with my parents not being from Birmingham, so I didn't have the local accent. As a child I had a northern accent, as both my parents were from Lancashire; but when I went to a private school I began to lose any remnants of a northern accent. The year in London also helped.

I can only remember that this was the one thing about me that attracted the attention of our head stylist. Male hairdressers were just beginning to become very popular and were much in demand with the rich clients who loved being 'taken over' by someone who they imagined would transform them. So I was overwhelmed when he started to single me out. He assumed the role of Svengali.

He took me shopping for 'grown up' clothes (I still wore flat shoes, a tweed coat and shoulder bag – not his idea of glamour!). Then he oversaw what I was having for lunch, as I was still rather plump. The next step was to cut and colour my hair red. I had never had so much attention in my life. I was in heaven and in love. He counted every calorie that went into my mouth and when that wasn't having much effect he marched me off to buy the latest thing in torture for large ladies – the Playtex rubber all-in-one living girdle. I went into the changing room and heaved myself into it. It felt as though I was trapped inside a giant Marigold rubber glove; but anything to please, so I put my clothes back over the top and went out to wow my man! We paid, left and set off to the cinema. We spent every spare minute in the cinema in those days. I soon started to feel very uncomfortable and so hot I thought I would pass out, but I managed to stagger in the dark to the ladies' loo, where I tore off the crippling, hideous garment, only to find that I had got it on back to front – though, quite frankly, I don't think it made much difference! I stuffed it into my handbag: I couldn't face putting it back on. I crept back to my seat and whispered to 'the great man' what had happened. We went into such a fit of hysterical laughter that we had to leave the cinema.

We had such a lot of fun; in spite of his bossiness, he really only wanted to turn me into a glamour girl – for my own good (I think). It was a lot of fun for a couple of years, during which I suppose I did do some 'growing up' and experienced my first heart-break. He soon moved on to his next ‘victim’, who was truly a very natural beauty and very soon I was hoping to make my escape.

Gradually I seemed to be doing a few pedicures (the most hated of the therapist’s jobs) and manicures, but all the time I was looking for an escape route.

A New Beginning

We now had a television company starting up just out of town: Alpha ATV Studios; so I wrote to them offering my services. Not many people were aware of jobs in television. There had not been anything like it in Birmingham, and most of the staff had come from London to set it up and get it running; but even they were still very new to the industry. It was almost like writing to God to ask for a job, so little confidence did I have in succeeding.

To my disbelief and shock, an invitation to visit the studio and meet the Head of Make-up arrived the following week. Oh well, no harm in going; at least I would get to see a real television studio.

Oh the nerves, the excitement and the disbelief of friends. How I ever got there heaven only knows. The studio was in a very desirable area between the Gasworks and the HP Sauce factory in an old converted cinema. I think this made me feel slightly more at ease: it all looked so ordinary. I found my way to Security and was taken through what looked like a rabbit warren of corridors to a door under the stairs that had the magical words 'Make-up' on it. The door opened into a room full of lights, mirrors with pictures of real stars around the edges, and row upon row of make-up products. Strange smells of surgical spirit and methylated spirits hit my nose; a far cry from Elizabeth Arden Blue Grass. Very pretty girls were doing a variety of strange things like cleaning false beards to remove the spirit gum and modelling false noses with a flesh-coloured wax. That, I later learned, was used by morticians to build up faces on dead bodies who had been disfigured by road accidents. It was all so far removed from anything I had expected, but was so exciting that I nearly burst.

A very elegant bohemian woman in dark glasses and rattling with bracelets and rings shook my hand; this was Head of Make-up. Oh, this was much more my idea of what I wanted to do. She explained that in the afternoons, when

Lunch Box was over, everyone practised the art of disguise, character make-up, beard making, fake injuries, prosthetics and all the tricks of the trade that make-up artists may be called upon to do at a moment's notice. She asked if I would like to have a go at making one of these beautiful girls look like an old hag. Oh my God, I've blown it! I had only ever learned how to make ugly old women look a bit better. I have to tell this awesome woman that I didn't know where to begin. She kindly told me that one of the girls would give me all the necessary make-up colours and some guidance on how it is done. My legs were dissolving as I began.

Two weeks later I received a letter saying that there was a job for me. Had they made a mistake? How could they want me after the terrible mess I had made of the beautiful face that just would not age under my panicking brush strokes? I telephoned, to be told: 'Yes, we think you have good potential to learn, even though your first attempt was crude; you have an eye for what is needed, so come along on the 13th and start with us.' Oh joy, oh hell, they will find me out once I am there every day; it's just a fluke that I can never repeat. I was on my way for the rest of my life.

Bearing in mind that in 1955 television was black and white, I had a lot more to learn than just character make-up. I was on a 3-month probationary period and would have to prove that their confidence in my 'potential' was justified. I spent the first weeks observing and practising the art of covering up men's blue chins. The monochrome and studio lighting made even the most freshly shaved face appear to be a 3-day-old stubble. Then any dark areas around and under the eyes had to be treated with a very pale shade of make-up so that the bags and dark circles would not look like the result of a heavy night on the tiles. As well as this, a suitable skin tone to match the face would be applied to the rest of the face, ears and backs of hands. Then the face was well powdered to remove all possibility of shine, for as soon as the studio lights hit the face it will look like a sheet of glass or appear very greasy and sweaty. This would be fine if it all stayed put, but inevitably the artiste would go off onto the set and become either hot or nervous or both. This was the moment when the famous chamois leather comes into action. Having finished the artiste's make-up, I then followed onto the set with a box of everything. I needed to keep control of the shine with a chamois leather soaked in eau de cologne and wrung out till just damp, and a box of powder puffs. The art was to swing the chamois quickly round in the air to evaporate the cologne, so making it ice cold. It could then be pressed onto the sweating face and neck of the artiste to cool them down, so that re-powdering could take place. They still do this today, 40 years later. All of this on live shows could be hair-raising as the moment to bob in and mop up had to be timed to perfection as the cameras were cued on, the red light would appear and the stage manager would be screaming for the set to be cleared. This is not quite so nerve-wracking today, as most shows are pre-recorded, but the urgency is still there as time is money and no-one has built in make-up adjustments to the budget.

Our tools of the trade were very different from the world of beauty. We used very expensive artists' sable-hair brushes in a variety of sizes from very fine for eye make-up to broad, thick ones for applying the grease paints and pancakes that were used for television. Very expensive sea sponges were used for larger areas such as ears and hands. At this time men's hair was usually very neat from expert cutting at the barber's so, apart from making it tidy and maybe applying a little brilliantine to calm down flyaway bits, nothing more was needed.

The grease sticks were still very much the Max Factor theatrical variety, but the colours used for television were very strange shades of greenish, greyish brown plus the highlighter shades for under eyes and, in the case of older ladies, the lighter one was used down the nose to mouth creases and the frown lines above the nose.

The whole process of the make-up was like a patchwork quilt. Shading in the brownish colour under the cheekbone replaced blusher that would not show up on black and white; the whole make-up job on the face consisted of shading and highlighting, with great emphasis on dark eye liners, grey shadow and loads of false eyelashes. No female in my memory ever appeared without false eyelashes. At this time very few people outside the media wore such things, but they did eventually become very popular for evening wear, as did the endless false hairpieces which so many television stars used for their appearances.

Our daily bread was earned doing a show called *Lunch Box* with the glamorous Noelle Gordon as the hostess. This was a daily show with musical inserts from Jerry and his trio. My first real make-up on artistes was on the trio, amongst much piss taking and rude remarks about trainee make-up artists. They stopped me feeling so nervous because they were around every day, almost like family. This still doesn't stop the nerves when the big names eventually come to sit in your chair. In those days we did quite a lot of big variety shows and celebrity quiz games, so it wasn't long before I had my chance to test my nerves on a lady called Sabrina, the 'Jordan' of the 50s, who was famous for her 19" waist and 42" bust. She was very pretty and I felt pleased with her hair and make-up, if anyone would see it.

A glass tank the size of a swimming pool had been set up in our yard behind the workshops and it took the fire brigade 24 hours to fill it with water; the bottom of the tank was covered with sand and sea shells and a small boat wreck. For her part of the game show Sabrina (very scantily clad) was to dive into the tank and retrieve some shells from the bottom; the whole crew stood holding their breath waiting for her 42" bust to 'dive' OUT of her so-brief outfit. It didn't. On live TV that could have been a disaster.

Even so, *Lunch Box* was very exciting to one so new to the game. It had a live audience, which always adds atmosphere, and the show went out live. We in make-up had to be on standby behind the cameras in amongst the huge mass of cables and equipment, sound booms and lamp stands, which were all hazards; but we had to be near enough to the artistes to spot the sweat and race in with a chamois as soon as the camera was on someone else. The nerves were jangling if the audience laughed at a near-miss as the red light would come on the camera before the mopping up was complete and we would dash out of shot, which caused a lot of good-humoured jeers. The fear of doing this act soon became less terrifying as experience and confidence grew.

I was beginning to feel at home at the studios and all the crew became like family. After a late lunch in the canteen, where everyone on the show gathered and ate school dinner-type meals, I would return to the make-up room and start helping to do the endless cleaning up of towels, powder puffs and sponges which were all washed by hand; then all the brushes had to be cleaned in a special dry cleaning fluid called Inhibisol. Everyone had their own make-up place with a huge comfy barber-type chair set in front of a mirror surrounded by light bulbs, a counter full of pots and boxes full of make-up colours, and all this had to be tidied, cleaned and made perfect for the next artiste to arrive. Chamois had to be rinsed and rinsed in cold water and wrung out, then hung up to dry out. Pins, grips and rollers had to be sorted into neat piles and returned to the appropriate boxes. Combs and hairbrushes had to be washed and put into a sterilising box. All of these tedious tasks (so similar to a beauty salon) were so much more bearable because the purpose of the job was so exciting. Our eyes would scan the board with advanced information on programmes due to come in and our hearts would flutter when names like Alma Cogan, Shirley Bassey, Matt Munro, Dickie Valentine, Dusty Springfield, Kathy Kirby and even Vic Damone from the U S of A appeared.

Someone who made his first debut at this time on TV was Rolf Harris – he came to the Aston Studio to do a children's programme. The item was for Rolf to display and talk about a boa constrictor. The huge snake was placed across his shoulders and the cameras rolled -- and there on live TV the boa started constricting! There was nothing Rolf could do; he just kept talking and trying to finish his piece to camera, while being practically squeezed to death. There was a certain amount of panic while the director wound up the show and Rolf was extricated from the frightening grip of the snake. We were all very shaken to have watched such a terrible situation that could have gone so horribly wrong. I wonder if he would remember it?

After the big clean-up, the magic hour of practice would begin; learning how to do character make-up, injuries, scars, wounds, black eyes – all of this was dependent on light and shade as, of course, blood looks black on black and white television.

It was all much more interesting than cleaning up people's toe nails and massaging fat faces that would only be appearing at some 'special' function; those people were so grand in their own importance and lives, but looked down upon their hairdressers and beauticians as mere underlings.

Strangely, stars don't behave like that. They are often so nervous that they look to the make-up room as a haven of specialists who can make them look and feel wonderful and their appreciation would often manifest itself in boxes of chocolates, flowers or sometimes champagne.

Three months on I have reached a stage where my head of department feels confident that I am ready to become a full member of the team and be fully scheduled to cover all programmes. This now means working a 24-hour clock and our working lives were bound by studio requirements. This means being available 7 days a week for 12 hours a day on a roster basis, which allows a certain amount of time off. Even this was exciting; none of my friends could believe the demands this job would put on me. To work Sundays and late at night would be a huge inconvenience to our social lives, but it was all such fun. The Michael Bentine Show was very late on Sunday nights and we all hoped desperately to be rostered on to it. What a wild and zany night boring old Sunday would suddenly become. I could write pages just about this show alone, but I don't want to bore you. Clive Dunn, Dick Emery and Michael were about the maddest, most wonderful people we had ever encountered. Their sketches made the whole crew cry with laughter; some of their escapades were so outrageous that we couldn't believe the show would ever get transmitted because everyone was laughing so much, including Clive, Dick and Mike. They made a lot of it up as they went along (or so it seemed) and their ad- libbing was phenomenal and only the cleverness of their director, Dick Lester (who later directed The Beatles), kept the whole show from turning into an hysterical shambles. So much for Sunday working. It was a big improvement on anything else I might have been doing.

One of my nervous moments came soon after my acceptance into the department. The name Katie Boyle appeared on my schedule. Oh joy, I have really made it up the ladder! Ten minutes before her arrival I wished I hadn't. Busying myself with everything that I might need for her make-up, my inside was in an uproar. The famous beauty swept into the room wearing a bathrobe and a shower hat. I was trembling as I greeted her, sat her in my chair, adjusted the back rest for her comfort, smiling but appearing to show great calm, I removed her shower cap and placed it jauntily on the electric light bulbs which had been on for at least half an hour. Splish-splash, it melted all over the roasting hot bulb. The result filled the room with an acrid stench. My legs dissolved again. Katie Boyle broke into peels of laughter and was the loveliest lady that I have ever made-up. It could only get better.

One of the recurring messages throughout my career is that every production brings new artistes with very different personalities and every first encounter still gives me butterflies in my stomach. I suppose it is like stage fright for actors, but even after 35 years in the business I still experience the feelings that I had that day in 1955. I would love to know if this is common with most make-up artists.

This feeling can be prolonged. Not all actors and actresses are sweeties and some can transmit their own nervousness in such a powerful way that the tension as the make-up starts to be applied creates something akin to an electrical force, which can on occasions affect the whole make-up room. The atmosphere becomes so tense that it can affect people's work. It only takes one highly charged actress to turn the make-up room into a living hell. This can, of course, be caused by many other reasons. Premenstrual is the favourite, closely followed by a millimetre weight increase, then come spots, hangovers and a thwarted love life. All these things contribute to some very bad behaviour behind the scenes. This is where the test of your mettle as a make-up artist comes into play. Never mind your own talents with brushes, puffs and pins. Just make this lady feel better. Whatever the problem, it must be cured by the time she leaves your chair. She must feel all her troubles subside during her hour in your tender care. The fact that one feels like a piece of chewed string after her departure matters not at all. She is the one appearing on camera and she is the one who needs to look good. The qualities needed to bring this about are far more important to the job than anyone can ever explain to a trainee. It only comes with practice and confidence in one's own ability to deal with absolutely everything that the book can throw at you.

All this fun was brought to an abrupt finish by the sudden news that my mother had only a short time to live. I felt obliged to offer to look after her for what time was left. So I left ATV Aston with the uncertainty of what now lay ahead. I did have the option to return, but during my years absence I fell in love and got married and couldn't see the hours fitting in with my new life.

I had always looked upon work only as something to fill the time before I would get married. That's what was expected in 'those days'.

A False Start

My return to this world after a period of absence of 9 years was brought about by the break up of my marriage and the need to support totally my 9-year-old son. They were 9 years of which I could certainly write another book and so I will, but maybe another day.

My great good fortune came towards the end of my marriage from an unfortunate misunderstanding. I had been testing the water with the hope of trying to kick-start my TV make-up career just as a freelancer. I had been keeping my hand in on the beauty front by doing home visits for weddings and special occasion make-up, but this was not frequent enough to support me once I was on my own. I was able to fit this in around my son's nursery school times, but he was about to start at full-time 'big' school and I would have a lot more hours free to work. I had started by going to the ATV studios which by now had moved from the Aston gasworks part of the city to a very nice modern property in the centre of town and the company was re-named Central TV. Lynette was the new head of make-up and she made me feel very welcome. Most small studios used freelancers from time to time and she let me start doing occasional work on the old *Crossroads* soap. I was really enjoying being back when things took a huge upturn. Lynette called me into her office and told me there was a job coming up and she would like me to put in for it. She arranged for me to fill in all the relevant forms and even put me through a health and sight test; all I was waiting for now was the 'board' or selection committee interview.

A phone call from Lynette brought my high hopes crashing down. It had been found out by the Union boss that I had lapsed my union dues when I left. It had been brought to his attention by one of the make-up girls who wanted the job herself. Although she already was on the permanent staff, the job held a higher grade and she felt it was her's by right. I hadn't ever been aware that I should have continued to pay the dues as at that time I hadn't imagined that I would ever want to return. So that was that; Lynette was really upset and so was I.

After I recovered from this massive disappointment I had to start thinking about what else I could do. I wouldn't even be able to go back as a freelancer to Central as the atmosphere with the other girl would have been unbearable.

In this mood of despair it came to me that maybe there could be some work at BBC Pebble Mill. I knew nothing about the BBC studios, except that they were brand new in 1962 and were in a beautiful part of Edgbaston, just up the road from my son's school.

I sent off my CV and waited. I didn't hold out much hope, so I was really in the doldrums. Quite soon afterwards I received a letter inviting me to meet the head of make-up and have a look round the studio. I thought it was just a polite brush-off; lots of people in those days wanted to look round studios as it was still a great novelty, so I didn't have any high expectations in case they might be dashed again.

A Glimmer Of Hope

Gwen Arthy was a short, fat, unimpressive lady in her late 40s – not at all like anyone I had ever worked with before. She was completely natural with virtually no make-up and wore something that looked like a canvas sailing top (it *was* a sailing top) and trousers; so different from the glamour girls at ATV. This was a very noticeable difference throughout the make-up department: I think it could be called the 'BBC stamp'. All the girls had to wear these large blue smock overalls with big patch pockets on the front. It certainly created a business-like look. It was only later that I discovered how much everyone all hated them; they thought they looked like canteen ladies.

After Gwen had shown me round, we went to her office and talked about the possibility of a job. She reminded me more of a headmistress than anyone in make-up, but she had a very kindly disposition towards me and was very encouraging and explained that, in spite of my earlier experience, the BBC only employed people who had been through the London BBC Make-up School. These courses ran for 3 months but were only held when the Television Centre needed more staff and then, if there was room on the course, Birmingham was allowed to send someone; and then only if they passed the exams would they be offered a job. And at the moment there were no plans for a course for at least the next 12 months.

I felt such a mixture of disappointment and excitement. I told Gwen that I would welcome the opportunity to re-train and would wait until the next course started; she seemed very pleased that I had taken the news so well and went on to say that, because of my more mature years and previous experience, she thought I would sail through; also, she would try and get me in to do occasional freelance work as long as I didn't let anyone know that I was waiting to go on the school.

I returned home with my head spinning. How could I go to London for 3 months, even if they accepted me? But that wasn't going to happen yet, so I had to start working on my own plans to make sure that everything would be in place if ever that day came. For the time being I had my mobile work, which I must try to expand.

Boarding school was what I had always hoped for Mike; and, as an only child and with an absent father, I felt that he would benefit from the company of the boys and all the excellent sporting facilities that would be part of the life. I had his name down for Bromsgrove, which was not too far to go for speech days and sporting events; also he would have several days out when he could come home, so I needed to make life as easy as possible from the travelling point of view and as this school had a good track record I went ahead and made arrangements for his entry at 9 years old, hoping that my chance to go to London would coincide with him starting there.

It was such a juggling match and my nerves and emotions were stretched to breaking point. The driving factor was that I must get the job in order to afford the school fees and I could only do the job if he was away at school.

Gwen was as good as her word and did call me in to do some work on their day-time show *Pebble Mill at One*. This made it easy to keep away from the main make-up area and any awkward questions. There was a separate make-up room just for this show near to the area where it went out live so that the artistes could be on the spot and ready to go on at a moment's notice. Also, they were used to having different freelancers to cover this programme.

I loved it and it was more like old ATV with different acts and items of interest every day. It was very exciting never knowing till first thing in the morning who was on the show and, if the truth be known, at that time I would have been more than happy to just stay on doing that, since I was only a few yards from the school and I was always finished in time to pick Mike up.

That was until one day when Salman Rushdie came to talk about his new book. I was working on *Pebble Mill at One* that day. I didn't know anything about this man in my make-up chair; we had such a variety of people on the programme and many of them were not famous, so he was just another shiny head to powder. As always I was in the make-up room right up until we went on air and, as it was live, it was quite a challenge to find a corner on the sidelines and keep out of shot, ready to step in if any sweat appeared on the presenters when the cameras were not on them, and dab them with the cool chamois. On this day, when I looked outside I could see swarms of strangely dressed men with banners streaming into Pebble Mill Road . Even then I was too busy concentrating on my work to pay much attention. It was only when the item interviewing Salman Rushdie came on that this huge crowd of them outside started advancing on the building, shaking their fists and waving their banners. It was the most chilling experience of my life, partly because of the huge number of them and partly because there seemed nothing to stop them entering the building. Everyone was frozen to the spot and the poor interviewer struggled to appear as though nothing was happening. Fortunately, one of our security guards must have phoned the police and they soon arrived in some numbers and quelled the advance of the hordes. It wasn't until I saw the local news that evening that the whole story was explained. His book had made some insulting remarks about their religion and they had come to protest. I have often wondered why a man of letters and supposed intelligence such as he didn't realise that his 'Satanic Verses' would upset his fellow countrymen and how much it has cost this country to protect him from them. How unsuspecting we were in those days that this would become the norm.

I was still fighting a losing battle at home and hardly ever saw my husband, but the more I worked the more I was able to put all that behind me.

As I have mentioned, my Guardian Angel was never far away and, when the time came to move to London, Mike was happily settled at Bromsgrove Boarding School and I was able to give 100% to the fantastic new career that I was embarking on.

New Beginnings Again!

The BBC School of Make-up was in Kensington House at the back of Shepherds Bush. It was like stepping back in time to the 30s. Everything was so solid: the iron windows and heavy doors, big radiators that people now go to reclamation yards to buy. It was a working, living museum piece and just wonderful and, in spite of the rather industrial feel about it, the building consisted of mostly offices for the various programmes. There was a lovely lady who pushed a snacks trolley around at coffee time and tea time and served the most divine home-made cheese scones and butter which set us all up for the day – they were an absolute must!

Our teacher and mentor was Ann, who had been a make-up artist for as long as the BBC had been making TV programmes. Like Gwen, she wore very simple clothes and no make-up. I started to realise that it was an unspoken code of conduct to never appear like a cosmetic counter sales person. I must say I had never been too much into a lot of make-up as there isn't really time or money with a young child, and now in class we were continually practising our 'art' on each other, so our faces were being cleaned off all day.

The author in a bald cap

A big part of the course was learning how to make bald-caps, partial facial disfigurement, burnt skin and old shrivelled skin. I was in heaven: I hadn't realised that there would be so much new and fascinating things to learn.

Ann was like our best friend and helpmate. She was endlessly patient and could always solve our problems and get us to see how we could achieve the effect we were after. Every day was a new challenge.

The author made up as an old man

On some of the days we had another lady who came to teach everything about wigs and how to make them, dress them and clean and re-set them, as well as Marcel waving them. That was the most difficult and scary thing and we all hated Marcel waving. We had bits of hair that were very old and had obviously been used by many people before us. They were called wefts and would have been used as tie-backs on men in a period production like *Poldark*, where it had to look as though men had long hair. Anyway, these were the pieces we had to practise on and it is very easy to get the iron Marcel tongs too hot and singe the hair pieces; we were all nervous wrecks for the first few weeks until we became more adept and remembered to test the tongs on tissue paper before applying them to the hair. The worst part was knowing that by the end of the course we would have to Marcel wave a whole wig as part of our exam. Apart from that, I loved every minute of it.

Practice wig

The class was a really big intake of 25 girls, of which 20 would go to Television Centre, one to Northern Ireland and two to Nigeria (apparently the Government had sent them as they would be starting up their own TV broadcasting station). Then two of us were going to Birmingham Pebble Mill.

Learning how to make casts for prosthetic pieces

All the applicants on the course had to be 21 and have been in education up to A- level. After that they would have been on at least a 2- or 4-year course in Beauty Therapy, or an arts degree, or a drama degree that would have had theatrical make-up as part of it. So there were no dizzy airheads and everyone really appreciated how lucky they were to have been selected; there was a great feeling of complete dedication in all our class subjects.

The truly sad thing now is that there is no longer a school at the BBC and young hopefuls have to pay thousands of pounds to get any training in film and TV.

As far as I know, there are no TV companies offering any free training in any department, such as sound recording and camera operating.

I was only too glad that I had started so long ago before there was such a terrific interest in all things *Media.*As all make-up assistants have gone through the BBC make-up school, a great part of the stuff that they learn is period wig dressing and application. Re-dressing wigs after they have been worn all day and removing the awful glue that is used is a huge part of what is done after the working day of 14 hours and just goes on until everything is ready for the next early morning start at 6.30. This can often add a couple of hours to the working day. Hence my comments about stamina.

The amazing thing is, throughout my working life I can never remember anyone going off sick. We were all too busy or too tired, but enjoying our work so much.

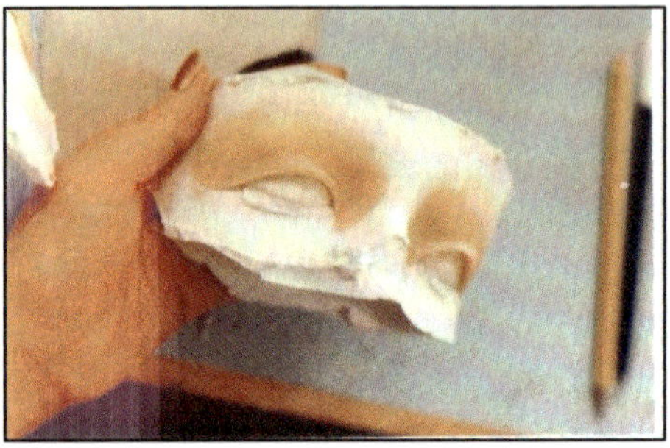

Modeling eye pieces for Geisha girl make up for our final test

Sadly, the BBC make-up school no longer exists, so the only way to get into the business is to pay huge amounts of money to one of the London Colleges which run a make-up course, but it could never give the rounded training that we received.

New Horizons

All my experience was gained in studio and most of the productions were under the title of 'Light Entertainment' or 'Quiz Shows', so when I returned from London BBC School of Make-up to Pebble Mill I was surprised to find that they did an awful lot more than *Pebble Mill at One*. I soon discovered that the bulk of the work was on drama, which meant spending a lot of time away on film locations. In fact, we hardly ever did work on the 'In-house' programmes: they had a make-up lady who was married and didn't want to go away from home and so it fitted her lifestyle perfectly as the show finished at about 2pm. Even so, I didn't really imagine that I would immediately be put onto the most prestigious programmes. I felt there would be a period of settling in and testing my abilities. From what I had heard talked about at the school, most of the girls who would go to Television Centre would spend their first year washing powder puffs, tidying cupboards and stock-taking, and if they were very lucky they may get to do the News Readers' make-up. I imagined a similar set-up at Pebble Mill. What I didn't know was that with such a small department there was no time to be a passenger. Everyone did everything and new trainees soon worked on main artistes' scenes; but that came later. When I started at Pebble Mill fresh from my BBC School of Television Make-up I was like the new girl all over again. I almost couldn't grasp my good fortune.

After the escape from a life of anxiety and divorce, I felt I was being allowed a chance at last to prove myself capable of a real career that would enable me to achieve a lifestyle that would support my son .

Starting At The Bottom – Again!

Pebble Mill was the most exciting production place that anyone could find himself or herself working in. The work was varied and challenging for those of us at 'ground level'; that is: Design, Costume, Make-up, Scenic Artists and Scenic Construction – the real workforce behind the scenes. The 70s and 80s were the golden days of television.

Well, good, in at the deep end, I thought, never dreaming that as well as washing the puffs, keeping the make-up room cupboards clean and stock-taking I would also be 'doing' *The Brothers*. There it was on my row of the schedule on the wall in the office. The office was very grand and had huge windows that overlooked the beautiful leafy Pebble Mill Road and Cannon Hill Park. We all had to report to the office to our Head of Department and check our duty rosters for the week ahead. My knees went to jelly; what could it mean? In my column: *The Brothers*. It was a series/soap that had run in the 70s for some considerable time. You will only remember it if you are over 50. I had always made a point of never missing the Sunday evening drama and it was high of my list of television favourites. I approached my Head of Department at her desk and asked if the schedule was correct. She smiled and said, "Oh yes, Maggie. We feel from your previous experience and age that you will cope with drama very quickly and soon learn about continuity from studio to film."

Oh great, I smiled back, hoping my shaking legs weren't showing, and fled back down to the make-up room, to the safety of a bucket full of soaking powder puffs, and I vigorously washed them while my mind whirled around the forthcoming new series of *The Brothers*.

Now calm down; I'm sure to be doing make-up on only the very minor actors with very small parts. Wrong! A few days before we went into rehearsal, the Make-up Designer held a seminar to discuss with the assistants on the show who would be doing what on the day.

"Maggie, I thought as you have some experience it would be nice if you take on Jean Anderson."

The room spun, my heart was pounding; she couldn't mean me, it couldn't be real. Jean, the matriarch of the show, the leading lady. Oh my God! I can't cope! Should I resign now, should I just be ill. Please let this not be happening.

"Oh, you will love her, Maggie, she's a darling. So easy: just a hair wash and rinse. I'll give you what we use, then set up on medium rollers. Nothing could be more simple and then just her usual make-up. Again, I will give you what we use on her and the make-up notes. We will be going onto film on location from this studio, so don't forget to take … the Polaroids … as relevant to the shooting script as the filming isn't due until next month. We must … keep … the continuity very carefully."

Oh my God, she doesn't know I've never done this before. What on earth am I going to do?

"Oh yes and, Maggie, we've got a new character in this series. Liza Goddard will be joining us and I thought you might like to do her as she isn't in too many scenes. I think it would be nice for you to do her as well. …"

It was just getting worse and worse; another hugely famous person.

"And maybe I will give you Colin Baker who plays Paul Merroney; he's a sweetie and won't take much time once you've got his hair under control. He hardly has any make-up."

Oh really? I am sitting smiling and nodding like a dog in the rear of a car window. Can anyone tell what is going on inside me? Well, what did you think the job was going to be? Pull yourself together; you've got four days to learn continuity from someone. Don't make a fool of yourself; you need this job.

Jean was indeed a sweetie; she couldn't have been more appreciative of what I did for her. The lilac rinse looked great; so did the make-up, which was like painting by numbers from a sheet of notes given to me by the Designer. Oh God, get my make-up place sorted out – it looked like a child had been let loose, throwing around colour palettes and sponges, rollers,

pins, brushes, combs, cotton balls, lipsticks, mascara. It was chaotic and Liza was due in three minutes and I had to have all her make-up out and ready to go.
Liza, in my whole career you will always be my favourite: you made me laugh so much when I was feeling so frightened; you were the ultimate tonic. You turned me around and helped me to love my work, not fear it. We romped through six hair changes per studio and still managed to have the continuity pictures and repeat the hairdo's for film. You and Colin made me happy to come to work. I couldn't wait for studio days, which we always seemed to spend crying with laughter and always getting the hair right just in time for your scenes. Do you remember your 'wedding day' to Paul Merroney in a force-8 gale with your veil and dress blowing vertically until someone put rocks round the bottom of your dress and I pinned the veil to your dress and somehow it all looked great on camera? Happy days.

Onwards And Upwards

So now I am one of the family…

We were all sad when it ended, but my visit to the office now reveals that my next production will be *Poldark*. I can now really enjoy the feeling of anticipation of working on a high-profile production; acres of preparation, mountains of wigs to be dressed ready for huge numbers of supporting artistes, extras who must all look as in period as the main artistes. Research of hairstyles in Corsons, the bible of period hairstyles. Men's facial hair and half-wig tie-backs all had to be prepared ready to go to Cornwall to shoot the exterior scenes, which would be done before any studio work.

We would be staying in Lostwithiel, which would be the central base from where we would travel with the artistes. We had several huge skips full of every possible thing that could be needed to set up a make-up room in the hotel that would be used at the start of every day to transform the actors before they were taken to location; then we would quickly pack up our own kits to be ready to follow them. Also, before we went, the main artistes came in to Pebble Mill for wig fittings and make-up tests so as to leave nothing to chance on the first day of filming. *Poldark* was another firm favourite of mine on Sunday evenings, so I was very familiar with who was who and even without their wigs and costumes they were recognisable, so it came as a complete shock to me when

Filming a scene from 'Poldark'

Captain Poldark (Robin Ellis) in person came into the make-up room looking for his make-up artist. I turned into a complete gibbering idiot. I've heard of being star-struck, but never experienced such a shocking state of ga-ga. He was perfectly relaxed, charming and normal. Why was he capable of reducing me to a love-sick teenager in two seconds flat? I will never know, but in some way it took away some of the pleasure of working on the show because I could never behave normally in his presence and he used to tease me a lot about blushing; but soon we were all too busy to carry on such silliness.

The stagecoach from 'Poldark', and my son!

We were a large number of make-up personnel with such a lot of main actors as well as hordes of supporting artistes. So we were all booked into pubs in the area and our make-up room was in the main hotel/pub in Lostwithiel. They were such happy days. The cast were a great bunch of people and made the long hours of work very enjoyable, as well as being in the glorious Cornish countryside in spring.

The massive scale set-ups on a popular series like *Poldark* come as close to feature films as it is possible to get for television. There are all the period carriages and people who own and usually drive them who have to be made-up with facial hair and tie-backs and costumes. This is a whole way of life for them and they are in constant demand. They spend their whole lives around film sets. Their skill in manoeuvring the huge horses and carts, wagons and carriages is spectacular, especially when they have to keep doing take after take and getting the animal and vehicle back on their marks to go again, involving the most intricate manoeuvring. I think there are very few people left who can take over such work.

Then come the stunt men, another brigade of such unusual and fearless skills and talents. They earn vast sums of money putting their lives on the line on a daily basis. Nothing is left to chance and they rehearse until they are stunt perfect. Even with all their body armour on they are still as agile as monkeys. 'On a night shoot one of them had to fall from the battlements at St. Maws Castle on to what looked like a pile of cardboard boxes - it was just that! It is so fascinating having all this going on around you.

Then come the huge design set-ups which are executed with military precision. 'The Boys' scene crews usually go a week or two in advance of everyone else, depending on the size of the production. They transform whole villages and town streets to the appropriate period and this involves painters, chippies and scene crews. Residents of the streets to be used are approached and paid to agree to have their houses decorated for the look needed and then they will be redecorated back after the filming is over. All modern exterior signs must disappear, either by setting trees and shrubs or painting over them. Red phone boxes cause a lot of problems, as do television aerials, phone lines and double yellow lines.

Sheets of rubber cobblestones would be rolled out like carpet and vast quantities of peat would be thrown down over white and yellow road markings. Branches of trees would be lashed to television aerials. It was so fascinating seeing the tricks of the trade and being part of it all.

Then came the supporting artistes who, for this production, were going to be local people. This is very unusual as unions usually only allow people with Equity cards to perform in this work and in these days it is a very closed shop. I am not sure how they got away with using locals, but they were such fun and they threw themselves into it with such enthusiasm, which was often very uncomfortable for them. On one occasion, 80 of them had to be made to look like beggars for a big market fair day. They had to be covered in make-up dirt, their hair matted with Vaseline and Fullers earth, their teeth blackened out with tooth enamel (which tastes foul), then they had to have sores of scrofulous (rice crispies) stuck round their mouths and noses with surgical glue. This sort of make-up is great fun to do but hideous for the recipients, but they were so good and just didn't mind what horror we created on them – they just loved this chance to take part in local history.

Vast tracking was laid around this huge fair day for the camera to move with ease amongst the stalls and crowds. The stalls had all been built by the scenic crew and all the produce and food items on sale had been made by a local baker to look exactly how food looked in the 1780s. All the pies and pasties, bread and rolls looked authentic.

Every department had worked round the clock to get this huge set-up ready for the action. Vast amounts of money had been spent and no area had produced anything less than perfect. The camera rolled, action was called and down came the rain; Cornish rain in spring has to be seen, but the show had to go on. The costume assistants had to stand holding huge umbrellas over the main artistes until the camera was on them, but the poor local supporting artistes had no such luxury. It was unimaginable that any of their make-up or wigs would survive this deluge, but in fact they did and the beggars looked even more authentic then before. The bedraggled look from the rain was wonderful, but the poor old pies and pasties started to fall apart, only to reveal their 'fillings', which were made of newspaper. Somehow, after a lot of patting dry, the people and the pasties went on film and looked fine on the day.

I felt that with all the experience I had gained on this production I could now feel confident of anything that would be asked of me; but there will always be something new, some unforeseen difficulty that will stretch the nerves and shake the confidence.

When we returned to Pebble Mill to start preparing for studio, I found I was to be doing a 100-year make-up on one of the cast. Fortunately, she was an older actress, which gave me a good base to work with and in those days we always had time to have some practice make-up before the day; but the hour-long make-up, layering fine plastic especially made for ageing make-up and drying each layer with a hairdryer, is very unpleasant for the actress and then the removal at the end is almost worse.

When we started on the scenes in studio we had some extra characters who had not been used on film and one of these artistes was Christopher Biggins, who was playing the part of a very frisky 'Reverend' Ossie Whitworth, who was up to no good with one of the Fair Ladies in the story. We, of course, had no idea that he would eventually become a National Treasure in *I'm A Celebrity, Get Me Out Of Here*, but even way back then his wonderful disposition shone out. He was the sunniest, most cheerful person and had the most uplifting effect on everyone around him. He is also a great entertainer and there was never a dull moment when Biggie was in the make-up room; he used to have us all crying with laughter. I was not surprised to see him overcome such ghastly challenges in the jungle and become chosen as The King by the whole country. It couldn't happen to a nicer chap.

Another extraordinary thing occurred at the start of our studio work on *Poldark*.

I was doing some shopping in my local supermarket and the lady on the check-out said she had seen me at Pebble Mill. We were always having parties of people shown round, so I asked her if that was what she was doing there.

"Oh no," she said, "I came to see my nephew; he is in *Poldark*."

Imagine my shock when she said he is Kevin McNally. Kevin was playing the young romantic lead. Up to that moment I hadn't known that he came from Birmingham and the connection with his name had never occurred to me. Just briefly I had thought he was probably one of our supporting artistes, but fortunately something stopped me from saying so. McNally was my ex-mother-in-law's maiden name and, to cut a long story short, after we had talked some more we realised that he was my son's second cousin. When I saw him next day I told him about it and we had a great laugh.

I did have one bad experience on Poldark. We were scheduled to do a shoot on a Tall Ship (a typical ship of the period) They were moored in Charlestown near St. Austel. They were manned by a group of young men on a training school and were completely perfect replica's in every detail. What we didn't know was that they have NO ballast or buoyancy and the allotted day would be a force 8 gale. Everyone was sick, even the crew. It was a disaster, the ship corkscrewed and pitched, I was so sick someone tied me to the side of the ship so that I wouldn't fall off whilst chucking up. I was carried off. The Coast Guard was angry that we had been sent out but it was too late by then. I wanted to DIE.

A Step Up

My first production working as an Acting Senior Assistant was to be on *All Creatures Great and Small.* Up until then I was really only classed as a trainee, but because of my previous years working for ATV I was treated as a fully-fledged make-up assistant, so the quick rise to Senior was very unexpected and rather exciting. A Senior is the designer's right-hand as she has so many responsibilities, such as liaising with the producers, director and artistes, working in London at meetings about decisions for the look required for the production, taking artistes for wig fittings, arranging make-up tests for any complicated set-up required in the story line, i.e. injuries, ageing, stunt doubles. Every script contains different requirements and has to be studied in minute detail to make sure that every eventuality is covered and to ensure there will be no hold-ups over the filming when studios go into production. In those days we were given plenty of time for preparation and rehearsal and there were technical runs before every studio. These were so valuable from everyone's point of view and were attended by all the Heads of Departments such as Lighting Director, Costume Designer and Set Designer. Everyone benefited from the opportunity to fine tune their own angle by watching the actors in rehearsal and making notes on the various timings that scenes took and what special effects might be required by sound or lighting. These preparations were what made the BBC so famous for its standards of excellence. How sad that it has mostly been swept away by the pressure of cutting back on budgets and doing less of the performance in studio.

The Senior Assistant is responsible for all behind-the-scenes preparations: ordering make-up; preparing all the wigs for supporting artistes; showing any trainees how to pack the big basket skips with everything that will be needed during the weeks of filming; making sure their own make-up kits have absolutely everything in working order with their electrical equipment, Carmen rollers, hair dryers, hot brushes;

ordering packs of film for Polaroid cameras to take continuity pictures. There have to be lists and lists of all the things to be checked off.

The worst thing that ever happened to me was managing to leave all the main artistes' wigs behind in one of our locked storerooms. I was by now the Designer on this production and so I had hoped that the Senior had arranged the transportation of them, but when we arrived somewhere in the Potteries we discovered that they were not with us. As they wouldn't be used until the next morning we were able to ring base and get them brought up, but it was a very close call, especially as our mornings started at 7 am and they had to be set out on blocks overnight so they wouldn't look squashed after travelling in boxes. We had a very late night trying to prepare them for the next day.

A lot of the time that is spent by costume and make-up is in preparation. Each actor may only be with you for 30 minutes, sometimes one hour, but the rest of the time is spent just being there to make sure that everything looks how it should through rain, wind and shine.

There is very minimal make-up used on actresses for period productions; it is usually what we call corrective make-up and definition, so that if an actress has any blemishes they must be kept covered up and, as we all know, they don't always stay covered up, especially if the weather is cold and damp. It wouldn't look too good in romantic scenes if the leading lady had a red nose or spots. Sometimes, if it is very cold, it can make their eyes and nose run, so we have to be there with tissues at the ready every minute that they are on camera. On one occasion on *Poldark* the young actress was doing her scenes barefoot on the beach and she was so cold that the costume department got a hot-water bottle for her to hold underneath her costume, but even that didn't stop her eyes from crying and in the end the director had to call a halt because she was just shaking so much with the cold that her nose and eyes were streaming.

The definition of make-up is usually a very little eyeliner and a shadow in a soft grey or brown in the socket and a light brush of mascara if it is needed. A lot of younger actresses hardly need anything, but a little blusher works wonders with most faces. The most worrying things are beards and moustaches that can so easily come unglued; some men seem to have something in the skin that repels the spirit gum that we use to put them in place. It may be that it is just sweat that makes them come unstuck, but it is always a worry when an artiste has the full works of sideburns, beard and moustache. The other thing that gives us headaches is a hat being taken on and off, especially if it is on top of a wig. Some of the period hats are extremely hard to fix on because they are made of such strong materials like woven straw and it can be very hard to push long hat pins through, and there is always the fear that if pushing too hard they will go into the actress's head; so this is another very time-consuming part of the make-up artist's work. I always felt if it had been the costume department's job to put the hats on they wouldn't have made them so difficult, but, of course, as with the hairstyles, they had to be made in the fashion of the period. The poke bonnets were the best – at least they tied under the chin.

Stunt Doubles and Transformations

I was never happier than when I was confronted with look-alike situations. So many storylines call for stunts and the men that do them come in all shapes and sizes. They do try to match them as far as possible to the artiste concerned in the action, but sometimes it is just not possible. We are usually forewarned about stunts and given a picture of the stuntman or woman with whom we will be working so that we can look out a wig that will match the actor (if possible). We had a good wig store at Pebble Mill and could usually find something appropriate. On one occasion we were away from base in the Cotswolds doing a murder mystery called *Cotswold Death* and it came about that there was going to be a stunt with a helicopter that hadn't been foreseen and the 'stuntman' in question would be the helicopter pilot. He was to double as the petite Asian lady who was going to make her escape in the chopper. He was about 6 feet tall and big. We found a long dark wig that barely fitted him and Costume somehow got him into a dress that hardly did up down the side and a large floating scarf that we wound around his head; but the killer was his shoes. Somehow Costume had got hold of a pair of size 10 shoes with high heels. The sight of this large man in all these bizarre clothes staggering like a drunk on the heels defies description – it was just too impossible to believe it would pass muster. However, as on so many occasions, with the art of camera work and editing all that was seen was a fleeting glimpse of a dashing figure in dark navy getting into the helicopter. The great end to that day was that we were given a fly round the Cotswolds. It was so beautiful. I had never done it before and never have since.

This week I have been enjoying the *Country File* summer show on television and for the first week the story centred on the Dales and James Herriot and the cast of *All Creatures Great and Small.*

It inspired me to write this account of the making of the series from my point of view, since most people wouldn't realise that the make-up behind the scenes could be such fun and so challenging. It certainly stretched our imagination in the most creative way and I have rarely been called upon since to reproduce such unbelievable numbers of animal injuries. It made me realise that there is still a lot of interest in the Dales and *All Creatures Great and Small* and it was so tear-jerking to see the cast all sitting round and remembering their days together on it and so I thought that is only half the story – so here goes.

é

The First Series Of 'All Creatures'

This was to be my first shot at 'Acting Senior' and I must confess it still gave me a buzz to be considered for such a high profile production.

Christopher Timothy and Carol Drinkwater

We knew it would be Wellies All the Way, but the opportunity to see 'THE DALES' at close quarters made it a very desirable show to be working on, and so we set off in extremely high spirits in our hire coach which, as far as terrain allowed, would go with us everywhere. The driver had become a friend from doing so much of our filming and it was his own coach company, so he had purchased all the latest music tapes. He had all our favourites and knew it would keep us very cheerful on our long journeys up and down the A1 – so off we went.

The view of fields surrounded by stone walls looked like a patchwork quilt unfolding on both sides of the road as we drove along through the Dales. I appreciated this open aspect of the countryside so much having travelled a lot in Cornwall, Pembrokeshire and Jersey, where the hedges make the fleeting sight of fantastic scenery a very frustrating journey, ever hopeful that round the next bend the so-longed-for scenic opportunity would be there. Not so in the Dales; here you have the feeling that every mile travelled is an orgy of beauty that you can wallow in as you travel, soaking up countryside that you already feel a part of even though you may never have been there before. It is there in your face and very quickly in your heart; it feels as if nothing has changed in England for centuries and that it will go on looking the same forever. There is still cow muck in the yards, however much time has marched on. Even over the 30 years since we were all there to make a series for television, I don't think the overall appearance of the Dales has diminished in any way. I was not prepared for the breathtaking scenery and the real feeling that time had stood still up here in these beautiful Dales. Around every corner as we were swept along in our hire coach there were more and more stunning views.

On every show there are several people in every department. Ours consisted of only three: the designer, me and a trainee. We would have our work cut out on busy days, but could rely on staff from Pebble Mill coming up for really big scenes with large numbers of supporting artists. Our trainee was fresh back from the London School and couldn't believe her luck to be on such a fantastic production so soon. She wasn't so thrilled when she found that she would also be doing 'short back and sides' hair cuts in vast quantities on all the men!

I must tell you about the coach which was to be our 'home' and often make-up room for the weeks and months ahead. Although we were all booked into some lovely bed and breakfast places and sometimes hotels, when we had done our artistes' make-ups in the 'Village Hall in Reeth' and set off for the day to the many locations, we then relied on the coach for doing many of the changes or repairs needed to the artistes' make-up and costume changes, as well as everyone having lunch at the tables on the coach.

As everyone knows, Christopher Timothy, Peter Davison and Carol Drinkwater were with us all the time, since most of the storylines required them to be ready for their scenes all day. My main responsibility was Chris and Carol. How lucky was that? They soon became my dearest friends and keeping Chris's period haircut neat was really the most make-up I needed to do for him. We were really aiming for the totally natural country look and with Carol it was a matter of controlling her beautiful natural curls into a slightly more old-fashioned look. So, apart from hats on and off and making sure that wind-blown pieces of hair were in the same place for continuity, the actual make-up job seemed pretty minimal, until we realised that every storyline had an injured animal in it and that my Designer and I would, as far as possible, be doing them!

The 'All Creatures' Car

What we didn't know was that every animal injury in the storyline would require a lot of attention from the Make-up Department. It soon became very clear that we were going to have our work cut out to achieve some believable looking animal injuries and other problems that I will now relate to you.

Another lovely job that came our way was mud – on and off at all relevant times, i.e. when an artiste slipped over in a cowshed or an animal had a sudden and unexpected movement that made the artiste get dirty. So, at the start of every day we had to mix up our bucket of artificial mud that went everywhere with us, just in case! That was not the worst thing we had to produce. Every day the script would throw up things like puss in the horse's hoof which had us propositioning the catering wagon for a mixture of mustard and mayonnaise which we then put into the hole in the horse's hoof that the real vet Jack Watkins had cut out in readiness and then we put some of the horny hoof bits back over it so that when Chris (Mr. Herriot) started to use the hoof implement the puss would ooze out.

Mostly we always knew in advance what would be needed from reading the script, otherwise we wouldn't be able to be ready when it came to that part of the day's shoot. We always had a gallon of artificial blood with us, but there were occasions when we couldn't foresee an event that would require our 'expertise'. One such day was a storyline about a cow that had calved and the afterbirth had not gone back as it should. As always, we had our vet Jack with us to guide Chris with what this procedure would be, but we (the Make-up Department) didn't think we would see anything except the back of Chris's shoulders doing some pushing at the rear end of the cow. We were miles from anywhere off up into the hills at a remote farm; we couldn't just pop to a butcher and ask for some offal that could pass for a cow's afterbirth. The director was insisting that he wanted to see the whole thing. We were trying to think of something that we could use that could be smeared with blood and hopefully pass for the real thing. We were frantic. We knew from Jack the vet that it should look like a wobbly bloody mass about the size of a football, but what? We just hadn't got anything with us. Then the Sound Department boom operative suggested that we could fill up a condom with water and smear blood over it. Great! There would surely be someone on a film unit with a condom. Well, no; but by great good luck the Sound Department always carry some to put over the boom when it rains. Praise the Lord.

Peter Davison as Tristan after an explosion

We managed with some difficulty to fill one with water and the real farmer's wife who lived at this farm gave us a tea tray to carry it on. We smeared the blood all over it and presented it to the waiting director, who seemed pleased, and

Jack gave it his blessing. Chris took up his position at the cow's bottom and manoeuvred the tea tray nearer and nearer to the correct position; there was a nasty 'pop' and a very big 'slosh' as the condom burst and poured its mess all down the front of Chris.

A birthday drink on 'All Creatures'

This sort of crisis is never allowed for in a tight film schedule as it will waste the time of about 60 personnel all involved in the shoot while the artiste is cleaned up and another condom is prepared. The tension and stress factors become unbearable, especially as this is the last condom that the boom operator has with him. Thankfully it all went without a hitch on the second attempt. It is very hard to explain how badly anything like that takes up time in the Make-up Department. Directors will go for take upon take for a variety of reasons, like a small sound or something in the distance that is a modern piece of equipment or if the sun goes in or comes out. There are many reasons for going again, but if it is to do with make-up it becomes a big problem of time-wasting, however necessary the work is. The same applies to costume changes; there is always the utmost pressure to do it in double-quick time. It is a very annoying aspect of the job because no-one does their best when this sort of impatience is being applied.

I would love at this point to take a break from the filming to add a bit of behind-the-scenes human interest.

Some Unexpected Situations

Our very first block of filming was scheduled for 6 weeks during the summer and my dilemma was that my 12-year-old son would be breaking up from boarding school and I couldn't bear the idea that I would be away for all of his holiday. By great good fortune the production team agreed to him coming along. I hadn't really thought what he might do every day and was worried sick that he would have a miserable time.

I should not have worried, as the whole unit took him as an equal. The film unit found him all sorts of jobs, from carrying the track for the 'grip' who does everything for the camera operator, to the caterers who were with us every day and who got him peeling spuds: not exactly his favourite job, but he was just treated like one of the gang, which I am sure could never happen now. On one occasion when we arrived for two weeks filming we had been booked into a rather lovely old pub called The Punch Bowl at Low Row in Wensleydale. Unfortunately, there was a power cut when we arrived early in the evening and it was getting dark, so the manager was handing out saucers with candles alight so we could find our way up to our room. Again, my son was with me. We had brought up a couple of our suitcases, which we threw on the bed, and put the candle on the bedside table. I was desperate to go to the loo, so Mike went back down for the rest of the luggage. He was very quick and on his return was appalled to find the room on fire. He shouted to me in the bathroom and we quickly raised the alarm. What a start to a busy working week! The room was blackened because the table lamp that I had stood the candle beside was made of some polyamide material which looked like a solid glass mushroom but was in fact a very flammable plastic and the draught from us pulling the door to had blown the flame over enough to set it alight. What a lesson to learn. Because I had flipped the lid open on my suitcase, the whole top layer of clothes was blackened and unusable and the ones underneath just smelled, terrible but I just had to wear them. The leg pulling was awful, but the hotel was really kind and didn't make us feel like criminals.

On another occasion when I was on my own, I had a room in a B&B in West Witton. Once again there was a power cut (they were pretty common in those days). We had travelled early in the morning from Birmingham and then worked until evening light stopped us, which was quite early in winter. When I got to the B&B I was shattered and just wanted a bath and my bed. Well, I was used to managing candles without starting a fire, but I really wanted a bath, so the landlady said that it would be OK because the water was still hot enough. What she didn't say was the central heating was off and as I took off my clothes I soon realised the cold in the bathroom was unbearable, so I got into the hot water and sat there with my jumper on, shivering. I had never felt so hot and cold at the same time and when I finally got into bed that was even colder and I hardly slept a wink. The cold in the Dales is not like any cold I had ever experienced as a city dweller and it took a long time to get used to being out in it all day for 14 hours and night shoots, which we did do occasionally, were even worse. We were all issued with 'weather gear' by the BBC, but in those days (1978) the equipment was pretty basic and not really adequate, but the following winter we had all wised up and invested some of our own money in some better ski-type clothing. Our best buy ever was Moon Boots. How we ever got over the teasing from the hardier members of the unit, I'll never know. They never stopped making wisecracks about our 'ridiculous' footgear. Little did we know that they were a revolutionary form of insulation that allowed us to stand around for hours in snow and ice with lovely warm toes and on our next block of winter filming we saw a lot of moon boots appearing on the male members of the crew who had taken the mickey so much.

I would say that cold feet had always been the worst part of the job. It really starts to make you feel desperate after several hours in freezing weather when the feet begin to become so painful you can hardly think of anything else and with several more hours work ahead it can be very debillitating, so the moon boots were invented just in time. We never did seem to film *All Creatures Great and Small* in prolonged good weather.

On another occasion we were going to film a very big local Darowby Fair day with hundreds of supporting artistes, or extras as we called them in those days. They would all be local people who loved to be asked to take part in the filming, but of course it made a huge lot more work for us because all the men had longer hair in the 70s and we were shooting short back and sides period. Fortunately, in those days most people wore hats and caps, so we did manage to do a few 'tuck-ups' in the hats because you wouldn't believe how much men resisted having their hair cut so short. They really made such a fuss it made our work twice as difficult. Thank goodness the main artistes never questioned having the correct hairstyle for the period they are working in. We had been working from dawn to get everyone and the main artistes ready for the whole day's work and even the local brass band had come in for haircuts. When we all went outside the marquees that we were working in, we could see the clouds gathering and the sky darkening, so we dashed around putting those awful plastic rain hoods over everyone and then we had to give the band some to put over their musical instruments, just as the heavens opened. It was such a difficult day trying

Darrowby Fair day

to keep everyone dry in between shooting and rain storms with the rain hats on and off every few minutes.

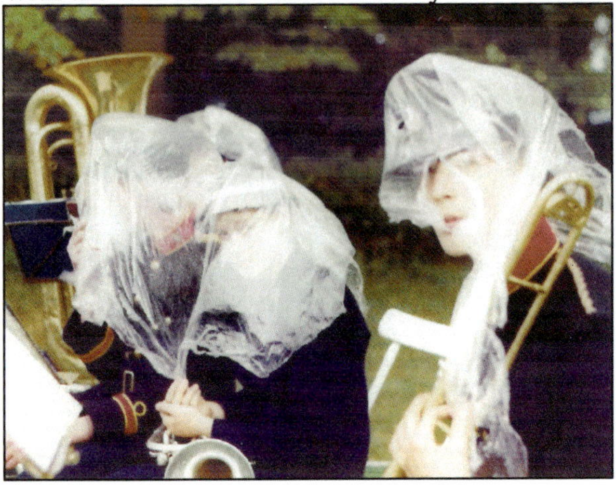

The Band keeping dry at Darrowby Fair

Luckily, we had been able to bring up extra staff from Pebble Mill to help us cover the extra work. It was so nice to see friends from home, but we didn't have much chance for any chatting until the day was over. As this day was nearly our last on this block of film, the producer decided to give us a party in one of the marquees after work, so they got us a mobile disco and the sparks put up some lights and the caterers provided a buffet and Production provided the booze. We always managed to find enough energy after work for a party, even though we were on our knees from the day's work. As soon as the disco started we were all up and at it, as were the field of cows that had heard the music and walked over to the fence just by the tent, and they all stood in a line swinging their bottoms and tails in tune to the music. One of the locals at the party said it was because they play music in the milking parlours as it makes the milk yield higher. It was one of the funniest sights I have every seen.

Very early on in the series we spent a whole day with a dead cow that Mr Herriot was supposed to find out the cause of death. The cow that was supplied had unfortunately been dead for some days. The smell was indescribable; since none of us had ever before been in such a situation we had not pre-empted what the day would bring. As well as the smell there were the flies, and the director, who seemed impervious to the stench, proceeded to take nearly all day to shoot the scene. He had long shots, close-ups, filming in a full-tracking circle round the beast, and we were a very silent group who left at the end of the day. We felt our whole bodies and lungs were contaminated from standing there for so long breathing in that smell. We all felt very sick, but, as always, a couple of pints in the pub soon put the roses back in our cheeks!

Speaking of roses, I must just tell you of the most delightful thing we discovered during our travels around the Dales. Near to where we were staying on one of our locations there was an old red telephone box and inside was a jar of freshly cut flowers. We started to check from time to time and the flowers were always there and always freshly cut. How great is that!

On another occasion we had the prospect of another rather unpleasant make-up to do on a little pony. The storyline said that his owner was abusing him and he had very bad saddle sores and some signs of being beaten. This presented a huge dilemma. How on earth could we do such a make-up? The Designer and I thought about it for days before the day of the shoot and decided we would just have to do it on a wing and a prayer, hoping the pony would stand still and that the mixtures of Kensington Gore (blood) and Fuller's earth would stay put where we wanted the damage to show. As a very desperate measure we had decided to take some Copydex with us, as some of the damage had to look like old scars. Thankfully, the pony was docile and the farmer who owned it held him still for us with a nose harness. Making any impression on his rather dense furry coat was really difficult. We were so relieved that we had the Copydex, as we were able to glue the coat into clumps and then put some of the blood into the gaps on the skin. The results were adequate and the vet agreed nothing more could be done, but we did not feel any satisfaction at what we had done and felt even worse that we had to walk away, leaving the poor pony with all the Copydex still in his coat.

Some days later I had to do an abscess on a sow's neck and again I had a lot of concerns as to how this could be done. I decided that I would make a prosthesis piece out of some cap plastic that we always carry with us, and spent some of my spare time practising to get the right size and inserting some coarse pig hairs into the piece, which was approved by the Jack. I then planned to stick this on to the pig with the spirit glue we use for wigs. On the day, it was pre-arranged that the sow would be in a horsebox, which made it easier to control her. Then the farmer held her in the corner with a sheet of corrugated roofing which I stepped over and performed my 'operation'. The prosthesis piece worked really well and I was able to remove it after the shoot. I got my confidence back on that occasion, which was rather a good job because there was even worse to come.

My next challenge was to be on a racehorse. They are extremely highly strung, as we had seen on several occasions on visits to film at racing stables. There are some very highly regarded stables in the Dales and it was always a privilege to be allowed onto such hallowed ground with a whole film crew, since the horses can so easily be spooked. They are so elegant and beautiful, rather like some of the best fashion models, and need to be treated with the greatest respect. When I knew that I was to do a make-up on the leg of one of them, my heart nearly stopped. Again, it was decided to make a prosthetic piece. The story was that the horse's leg had been ripped when it went over a hedge jump and the action was for the vet to go in to repair the damage. Even a real vet would feel anxious performing such a thing on a racehorse, so you can imagine how I felt. I made a lovely piece that looked just like a flap of skin to dangle on the horse's leg with some blood running down, but the thought of applying it was giving me the collywobbles.

On the day everything was set for me to go into the stable. All the cameras were in place and everything had been done calmly and quietly before the horse was led into his position in the stable, and then it was my turn. Thank goodness I had been successful with the sow, which gave me courage. It was fortunate that we had done a lot of prosthetics at the BBC make-up school, but nothing had prepared me for the nerves I felt as I approached the horse. As I went into the stable he snorted and tossed his head, his warm breath trembling around his velvet nose as he towered over me. I talked to him, told him how beautiful he was, stroked his beautiful silky neck and as I talked I smoothed my hand nearer and nearer to where I was going to stick the piece on his leg, moving lower and lower. I had applied all the glue and blood to the piece so that was all I had with me and then as I stroked him I just pressed the piece on the place below and held it for what seemed minutes. I can't remember taking my hand away or moving back behind the camera, but the camera was rolling and the shot was a huge success. I don't often blow my own trumpet, but everyone said it looked fantastic, so for once I was bathed in glory – a very rare experience – and my sense of relief was never so great. I can never see a racehorse now without remembering that day.

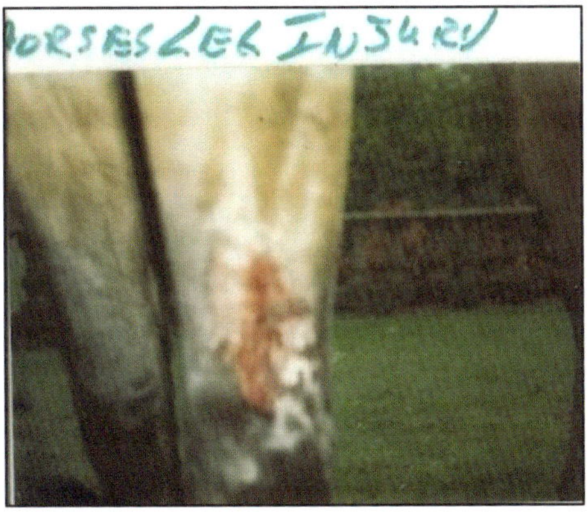

My next challenge was a racehorse!

A couple of us were billeted at a farmer's B&B in the village of West Witton. When we booked in earlier they had given us a front door key and, on one of our after-work visits to the local pub and after quaffing a lot of Old Peculiar, we rolled in late and there was no-one around. It was a very small cottage and we were the only residents, or so we thought. We crept up the creaky stairs with a lot of suppressed giggling and stumbled around, trying to decide which rooms we were in. At some point, having opened and closed several doors, we found our beds and slept. I was brought back to consciousness by loud banging and shouting, which seemed to be coming from outside my door. It was still dark and I leapt out of bed and went to find out what all the commotion was. There was a door opposite mine on the landing and the noise was coming from it; in my dazed half-sleep I could see that there was a bolt on the door in the locked position. I slid it back and shot back into my room. When we left in the morning there was still no-one around, but when we returned in the evening the lady who had let us the rooms said that her husband the farmer had been locked in the attic when he had come down at 5:30 to milk the cows. It looked as though we must have mistakenly pushed the bolt across when we were fumbling around trying to find our rooms. We explained what had happened and apologised for causing so much trouble.

During a very cold winter we were scheduled to do a night shoot in which Carol was to be present at a lambing – oh, what a long cold night that was! Thankfully, by now we had the famous moon boots.

It is on these occasions that all the crew really support each other. Lee Electric Northern, who supply all the big lighting equipment, really came into their own: they are as entertaining as stand-up comics and kept everyone cheerful with some terrible jokes; and the caterers kept us all plied with tea, coffee and soup. Kennedy's our caterers always did us proud. Every day was a banquet. We had a choice of two or three hot meals and pudding at lunch-time, as well as full-cooked breakfasts and trays and trays of sandwiches and cakes at tea-time. The amount of food is awesome (as my son had found out when one morning he couldn't get his jeans on) and when we do these all-night shoots there is another hot meal during the night. Generally there would be around 60 people at every meal on location and all this is prepared in the back of a kitted-out lorry. Nowadays they provide double-decker buses to use as dining cars so that everyone can sit at a table in the warm. Then we were lucky if the coach could be with us because it couldn't get near enough on a lot of the farms we worked on, so we just used to find a wall to sit on to have our meals.

On this night during our supper break we had some bin liners off the caterers and went tobogganing down the nearby snow slopes; it was a very welcome change from trying to keep warm and was a lot of fun. The main trouble with filming is that everyone has to stand perfectly still for hour upon hour in case it should spoil a piece of filming. The only time we get to repair any damage from wind or rain is when the lighting changes take place and the 'sparks' have to move all the huge brutes (lights) around for the next shot. Those filming lights run off a very big vehicle called the Genny, because it has a huge generator inside. This can be very useful to the Make-up Department because, if the sparks are in a good mood, they will let us plug our hairdryers and Carmen rollers in for a quick repair job; so we always try to stay in their good books in spite of the fact that they love to take the piss out of the Make-up Department and our moon boots, ear warmers and hand warmers, which are invaluable on night shoots. The hand warmers were invented for fishermen and are like large 'T' bags that are shaken to start them heating up. They do get really hot and can melt a tail comb in your pocket if you are not careful. This actually happened once.

The crew sunning themselves on the set of 'All Creatures'

There are so many things that we must have with us at all times and this is another of the nightmares of filming. The continuity camera with spare film is the most important and takes up such a lot of space, with all the script, pencil case, etc, and that is before I start on the make-up kit, hairdryers, hot brushes, gas refills, Carmens, etc etc. Well, I won't bore you with all that.

Eventually, after a very long night, one of the sheep started to go into lambing mode. I quickly got Carol who, fortunately, had been given a lovely big Tam-o'-Shanta that covered most of her hair and kept her warm, so she wasn't going to need a lot of maintenance work. They got her right on her knees at the rear of the sheep and the camera rolled. Unfortunately, Carol had never seen a lamb's birth before and she was so moved that the tears spurted out as she put her hands out to help the lamb. Of course, this wasn't wanted by the director who said, as a country girl, 'Mrs Herriot' would not be so emotional, and he made them do another shot with no tears and Carol just holding the little scrap of new lamb in her hands. Poor Carol, she had just become completely lost in the emotion of the moment and forgotten she was acting. I think we all shed a few tears as well.

As we soon found out, the softness of the scenery doesn't make for an easy life. Farming then and now is a 24/7 job and only the deeply committed can succeed on the roller-coaster that the work in farming offers, with so much hardship and grief that can happen overnight when foot and mouth strikes, as well as many other problems that can crop up in the health of animals, as we were soon to find out.

The farmers, at the time that the *All Creatures Great and Small* story is set, were always struggling to make a living. We didn't come across many farmers where money was no object, so the vet's was the last bill the farmer wanted; and yet the animal had to have treatment to continue being of use for the job, and so the Herriot stories are generally about hardship and hopes for everyone involved with keeping the animals fit for the job. This has proved to be a fascinating subject for the rest of the population, some of whom have never been on a farm.

We certainly had no make-up training that included animal injuries, so it was very much a combined effort of Jack the vet telling us what any given illness or injury would look like and how it would manifest itself on the animal. Like the purple diamonds on the sow's belly.

It happened on a day when my make-up Designer needed to go off-set, leaving me in charge; ;ell able to get on with anything required, or so I thought. It was a beautiful sunny afternoon and we were all returning to the farmyard after our lunch; there was a lovely relaxed sunny day feel about it all. The crew and director were positioning the camera and lighting around a very large sow in a stable when the director turned to me and said, "Shall we do the purple diamonds now, Maggie?" I looked blankly at him. Jack wasn't on set like he usually was when we had to do things like this, so I said that I didn't know about purple diamonds on the pig, I didn't remember reading about that in the script, and we hadn't made any notes for make-up requirements for such an illness. Meanwhile, the crew had all started tittering and my face was getting purple, when the director burst out laughing. "Just testing, Maggie!" I could have cried at being found lacking in the absence of my boss. I had felt the bottom drop out of my confidence to be there on my own doing the job. In the end everyone had a good laugh, but it made me always double-check on the script for the day's injuries on my watch.

Wedding Day rehearsals in the rain

During the blocks of filming we returned to Pebble Mill to film the interiors in Studio A. This huge drama studio was like an aeroplane hangar at the back of the building behind the plate glass windows that fronted Pebble Mill. Our make-up rooms were right beside them so that the actors could go straight in to perform their scenes and not keep anyone waiting. Studio time was so expensive and was why the building was eventually considered obsolete and not affordable. It would be hard to imagine what could be reproduced inside the vast interior of this void.

Preparing for the wedding

This was when the continuity pictures became so important; for instance, we would always see the vets leaving and arriving at Askrigg House, although we never ever went inside the real house on location and the costume and make-up had to match up exactly several weeks later when we saw them arrive back in the studio set of Askrigg House hall.

For *All Creatures Great and Small* there was the vets surgery and waiting room, the hall and dining room and the kitchen and living room at Askrigg House. As well as these there would be some of the interiors of the farm cottages that the vets had visited on location. Through the French windows in the dining room set was an area that looked like a garden with a piece of lawn made of artificial grass. At the start of a filming day, the family dogs that were always with Siegfried on location were brought to Birmingham for the studio and when they arrived they would dash out onto the 'lawn' and cock there legs up and wee; we were speechless the first time we saw them, but no-one seemed to notice what was happening.

On another occasion we had a dog who was a 'character' in the storyline and he had been brought down the day before by one of the location managers who was staying with our set designer; the house he lived in backed-on to Canon Hill Park opposite the studios and he managed to escape and run off into the park. It was panic stations and a news bulletin went out on the 6 o'clock news asking anyone who had seen the dog to contact Pebble Mill. Amazingly, someone had found him and had taken him to the local police station and he was returned in time to appear in his 'starring role'.

On another studio day the scene crew had built a full-size cowshed because something had gone wrong with a section of the film that had been done on location. The poor cows had had to travel on a very long journey because even they were 'period' cows with large horns, and they were the only herd that we were using for the filming that could be found, so they couldn't just get some local ones. When they arrived they must have been very tired and nervous as they were led into the stalls on the set, for there was a very loud sound similar to people clapping. We had gone to see them arrive and were horrified to see that the 'clapping' was the poor cows dropping their 'load', and that was what the sound was. The journey had given them nervous and upset stomachs, and the mess was terrible. I thought they got their own back for the terrible journey that they had endured.

Another huge set-up that the scene crew had to build was a very large drawing room for a scene with an eccentric woman who had about 50 cats living with her. We couldn't imagine how they could possibly control so many animals in the set, since cats are so agile and can easily jump over any barricades. Imagine our surprise to find that most of the cats were STUFFED, with only a few selected real ones for the action of the scene, andthese were controlled by a professional animal handler. It was so clever and they didn't cause too many hold-ups.

Unlike Mrs Pumphrey's Trickey Woo, which was a very spoilt Pekinese dog that was a regular on filming up in the Dales.

Trickey was the bain of James Herriot's working life. The dog was completely ruined by his owner, Mrs Pumphrey, who would give him chocolate to eat and then demand that a vet come out to attend to his upset stomach. This annoying task always fell to James, as Siegfried was the senior partner in the practice and considered it beneath him to attend to such frivolous matters. The actress who played Mrs P. was Margaretta Scott and she loved to come up from London for her scenes and we loved to see her. She was in her own life very grand and suited the part perfectly. She had some wonderful floating dresses to wear and it was such a change to have a bit of glamour make-up in amongst all the animal injuries. She was so beautifully coifed and was perfect in the part.

She was with us when we had the big Darrowby Fair Day and, of course, still had all the finery of a lady in her position, topped off by a large feathery hat and some very dainty shoes, even though it was to take place in a muddy field. Of course, the lavatorial arrangements for the day were primitive to say the least; just some Elsan buckets with some sacking round the outside and duck boards to walk on through the mud, but inside each one it was quite awful under foot. We were all hoping Margaretta would not have to pay a visit but, of course, she couldn't go all day and when the time came the Costume Department gave her some wellies to wear and so she managed to pick her way over, accompanied by her costume assistant. After a few minutes she was heard calling out, "Darling, there is no stationary in here!" Fortunately, her costume assistant quickly found a toilet roil in one of the other cubicles and saved the day.

I had my own lavatorial experience on an out-of-the-way location. As females we were very much in the minority and no special facilities had been organised for us; since we moved locations so many times a day it would have been difficult to always have a mobile one over some of the rough muddy ground. So we were expected to find a bush; but even these were never there when you wanted one and, because we were so bundled up in layers of weather clothing, removal of waterproof trousers over the top of jeans made it virtually impossible. So, after a week or two of difficulties, we did ask if something could be provided to ease the situation. What turned up was a very small tent with an Elsan bucket inside it. This they said could be taken with us to all locations. Unfortunately, it was even more difficult to remove the waterproofs in such a confined space, but we persevered and at least they had shown willing. So there I was with a great puddle of clothing around my ankles, sitting pretty, when the damn tent blew over and left me sitting there for all the world to see. I thought it must have been a gust of wind, until I realised that the two little boys running down the hill had let the guy ropes off.

Carol Drinkwater

Carol will always remain my favourite actress. She was a breath of fresh air; never moody or difficult, a warm, merry and very natural girl. I can remember our first day on location. We were only working with Chris and a cow, which had fallen and become stuck in a small byrne (stream), so Carol had decided to come out to watch and meet everyone. She hadn't got any scenes that first day, so she was dressed for the summer in her own clothes. The shorts she wore were kind of Boy Scout-cum-MASH ex-army drill, but on her figure they looked anything but. There was always an impishness about her and an air of complete unawareness of her own effect on men. The male members of the crew went into meltdown. She was oblivious, smiling and chatting to everyone, just enjoying the beautiful weather and getting to know who was who on the crew. They all remained in love with her for as long as she was the leading lady in *All Creatures Great and Small.*

Sadly, after the first couple of series, we were all disbanded and went our separate ways: me back to Pebble Mill straight onto another epic. I lost touch with Carol until many years later. Someone came to tell me she was in the bar (the great meeting place at Pebble Mill). It was soon my lunch hour and I flew over to see her. She hadn't changed a bit. She was now married to a French director and had come over to launch a book she had written. It was lovely to see her still so happy.

Chris also disappeared into his London life and I didn't see him again until I had left the BBC. He turned up in the road where I live while they were filming *The Doctors*, which is made in Birmingham in a nearby house. We fell about reminiscing and he took me to lunch at the local pub. He really hadn't changed either, except he seemed to be bigger than I remember, but then so was I.

Peter, dear Peter. He went off and did *Dr Who* and became very famous, but as soon as I met him again I knew it hadn't changed his view of himself or life. He was still just the 'boy next door'; even though he was a few years older, he still held that natural boyish charm without being a lad. He was just as charming to everyone he worked with and was loved by all. I suppose I felt more motherly towards him because he had been so great to my son on location; he was just like an older brother. So when I saw his name on my list of artistes to contact (I was by now a fully fledged Designer with my own shows) I was over the moon. The epic we were embarking on was Arnold Bennett's *Anna of the Five Towns*. Another period piece. When I got together with Peter to discuss his look for the part he was to play, we toyed with the idea that it would be a change if he had a moustache to add a bit of maturity and be more in keeping with the look of the Victorian era. There was going to be enough time for him to try to grow his own before our scheduled filming dates, so he said he would have a go, but didn't really think it was going to be very good, as he had never grown one before. So we arranged to meet again in a couple of weeks to see how things were going and still give me time to have some made if necessary. It is very much more comfortable to have a real moustache than a stuck-on job. Most men loathe having any pieces of facial hair stuck on and they are a nuisance to keep an eye on during filming. So I was very disappointed when a couple of weeks later I met Peter to see that it just wasn't going to be possible to use his own rather thin covering. But that's all another story.

Anna of the Five Towns was in a way a huge leap forward in the way we had always made drama productions on film.

It was probably the very first period drama to be shot on video and was viewed with extreme distaste by true 'film makers'. This was another move to try to cut costs on such huge-budget productions. I must say, it seemed a very short--sighted choice; when on location we now had all the cables from the cameras to the OB unit (a huge vehicle with all the technical monitors and sound equipment in) that were always taking time to accommodate and keep out of shot, but what did I know? The next production that it was used on was *Boys From the Black Stuff*, so at least I had got used to it by then; but It still never quite had that filmic quality of 65mm; and certainly never achieved the status of real film.

Anna of the Five Towns was lovely experience, filming all around the Potteries and a trip to the Isle of Man for a week's filming. Not a place I would ever have visited if it were not for my job. It was like stepping back in time and very hard to imagine what it would be like during the motorcycle races. It felt very peaceful when we were there, but rather depressing.

The next production with Peter Davison was about another two years after *Anna of the Five Towns*. It was to be a present-day story about life on a university campus: *A Very Peculiar Practice*. It was my first return to work after six months in hospital having a back operation. I had wondered if I would ever work again, but with great good luck I made a complete recovery. What could be better to break me in again but a very lightweight modern drama?

I acquired a small trolley to help carry my 'stuff' around and I think the many miles we walked around the campus at Birmingham University were very a beneficial exercise. It was an amazingly beautiful summer: the weather stayed fine for the whole of the filming and most of the locations were just down the road from where I lived.

Peter needed almost no make-up and our leading lady was very natural as well, so my workload was extremely light. It was just another very happy time in my life.

Working so much with Peter I almost started to feel related to him; he was the one actor in my whole career that was always popping up again and again. He was never moody or uptight. He had the most relaxed approach to life and any work I ever did with him was pure pleasure. I am often asked who was the best person I ever worked with and I always say Peter. He had a fantastic approach to his job and a great sense of humour.

I have said previously how he had been so great with my son when working on *All Creatures Great and Small*, but by now Michael was about 17 and very into composing music. Peter, who had the same interests, lent Mike an expensive piece of equipment to help with his music and then wouldn't hear of having it back. I have never forgotten his generosity.

Chris spent more time up in the Dales before we all went up because as an actor he had no experience of putting his arm up cow's bottoms, so he moved to the Dales to learn these 'arts' long before any of us. He never tired of telling people of his first attempt at the amazing 'arm up the bum'. He really enjoyed everything that the work demanded and never shied away from the most intimate and scary jobs that are part of a vet's daily routine. He really quite liked the feeling of examining cows' insides and there were no camera tricks: he really did put his arm right inside the cows, under, of course, the close supervision of Jack the vet. I imagine it must have been an amazing culture shock to be back in London permanently.

Chris did, of course, go on to do another series some years later with a different lady as Mrs Herriot. I was sorry not to be involved with it, but glad for the next lot of crew who would experience life in the Dales.

Robert Hardy as Siegfried was to me a complete enigma. He was always around for his scenes, but as the 'famous actor' on a location where he had only a rather smaller part to play he seemed rather remote. He would turn up in his Range-Rover, do his scenes and disappear, so we didn't really ever connect with him. Only the Designer, who did his very minimal make-up, spent 10 minutes with him on the days he came out. Also, he always wore a hat, so there was no hair continuity for her to worry about. Until one occasion at the end of the filming. It happened because a meal had been arranged for cast and crew to celebrate the end of shoot and for some reason it was about 15 miles from where we were staying. Heaven only knows how I pulled the short straw to be with Robert in his Range-Rover on such a long journey. However, he was utterly charming and chatted merrily all the way. I couldn't have felt more at ease.

The Cricket Match

Every episode of *All Creatures* had scenes at the front door of the 'Vets Practice' and so we became regular visitors to the house in Askrigg that was used for this purpose. When the filming crew came to the village with such a lot of personnel and vehicles the little village looked swamped, with the huge generator, props trucks and our coach being central to all the comings and goings of the actors. Because we had all our make-up and costume changes for the day on board, the villagers soon started to congregate to enjoy the spectacle; especially after the first series had been shown and some of them had seen their houses on the telly. We were made very welcome and started to feel quite part of the community, to the point when one day a representative of the church roof fund-raising committee approached us and asked if we would help out with a cricket match that was being organised the following month to raise funds.

The schedules were studied and it was organised for one of the Sundays that we could be up there on a day off. The crew and some of the actors would play the local team and, along with some other fund-raising stalls around the perimeter of the field, we 'the make-up team' decided that we would set up a stall offering 'glam' make-ups for the ladies and injuries or fantasy make-up for the children.

We were swamped with little boys wanting cut throats, black eyes, bullet holes, etc. The amazing thing was that when some ladies eventually joined the queue they didn't want anything glamorous; they wanted black eyes as well so that they could go and shock their husbands. It was all good fun and it really raised a lot of money for the new roof, but we were on our knees at the end of the day because the queue never stopped and the children were going off to show their long-suffering parents and then removing their 'wounds' and re-joining the queue.

Shall I? Shan't I?

After I had done my year of 'Acting Senior' on All *Creatures Great and Small*, I was encouraged to go for the next Promotion Board which involved going before three people from London and two from Pebble Mill to answer a lot of questions that would prove to them my worthiness to be promoted to Senior. My Head of Department was on the Board and I knew she was pushing for me. I did feel a bit nervous, but I also knew that if I failed I still had a job and I still loved it whatever.

Luck was on my side and soon all the paperwork to confirm my new status as SENIOR ASSISTANT arrived. Of course, I was ecstatic with relief. Apart from the increase in salary, I loved the extra responsibility that I would have and I was one step nearer to the ultimate goal of Designer.

I had no idea when I joined the BBC that I would ever be anything more than 'a make-up artist' and really didn't know that there would be this possibility to rise through the ranks to such heady heights. Having not being that bright at school had given me a self-image of low achiever, but I suppose as well as growing older the BBC had opened my horizons to unimaginable career moves. That was one of the BBC's areas of excellence; it was possible to start in the postroom and rise to any position that one's talents allowed.

And so for now I was very contented with my new position and, as it would only change if one of our Designers left, there would not be any chance of moving up in the foreseeable future. The shock came around a year later. One of our most highly respected Designers was going to live in Canada – WOW!

It was really a bit too soon for me to be thinking of applying and even then I would be up against people from other regions with more years of experience. A Designer's position was so rare that no-one ever gave up unless they died or had a better offer from a commercial company. So the heat was on and once again my Head of Department encouraged me to have a go, just to get the experience of taking the Board. Well, the rest is history. Strangely, there were not that many applicants from anywhere. I can't remember now just who, if any, but I did get through and did become a Designer, and it was everything that I could have dreamed of. It fulfilled every area of work that I had grown to excel in, thanks to the good old Aunty BBC.

From then on I just went from strength to strength, growing in confidence with every new challenge. I became a good communicator with the girls that I had to work on my productions and the directors and producers that I had to negotiate budgets and artistes make-up with.

My first production as a Make-up Designer was *Angels*, a hospital drama about young nurses starting their careers and the daily goings-on of the ward and their ups and downs in their private lives. It was very popular and had a big following of the young and not so young. Medical dramas in those far-off days were not so ubiquitous as they are now and still hold their fascination in spite of there being so many on the box.

Angels was considered almost as a training programme for all the technicians; as well as the young actresses' first television, the sound recordists and camera operators were given extra responsibilities. It was good to get to grips with all the paperwork, tech. runs and trips to London, talking the talk with producers, directors, and finding the way around Acton rehearsal rooms for the technical rehearsals that we had before every studio. It was this attention to detail that gave the BBC the upper hand on high standards and quality production.

Acton was the most exciting place at lunch-time, mainly because there were so many different productions being rehearsed on every floor and the canteen would be full of the most incredible variety of 'famous faces', from Sir John Gielgud to Bonny Tyler; every production of light entertainment or drama that was broadcast from Television Centre or Pebble Mill was rehearsed at Acton.

It may not sound like much fun catching the 7:10 from Birmingham to Euston and then a 40-minute journey on the underground to Acton, but I was floating on air. I never tired of those journeys which became such a regular part of my life, because it was so rewarding to have so much information about the work in hand. The young cast also loved to come to Pebble Mill for their studio days because the city and 'night life' was so close for their playtime after studio. Having worked until 10pm, they could easily get down to Broad Street to all the clubs. In those days it was safe and the night clubs weren't full of drunks. Bobby Browns, The Rum Runner and Mr. Moons were all fantastic clubs and we all joined in after we had cleared up the make-up room.

Back in studio A, the same challenges that had become a regular part of my life were the injuries and special effects make-ups that any medical drama require. On one occasion I was working on the face of a man who had supposedly gone through the windscreen of his car. I was totally absorbed with the detail of so many cuts and bruises that I had failed to notice that my subject had turned a funny colour. It was only when I noticed that he had started to sweat profusely that I registered something was wrong. I asked him if he was OK, but by now he was slumping down in the chair. I dashed to get some water and a cool chamois leather. After a few moments he started to rally round and told me he thought he had become faint because of the horrible appearance of the make-up that I was creating on his face. I felt quite pleased that it was looking so realistic. What more could I ask?

Angels ran for about 12 months, with filming at a hospital in London and alternate weeks in studio and by the end of it I felt very confident that I could meet the demands of most situations.

Sophia And Constance

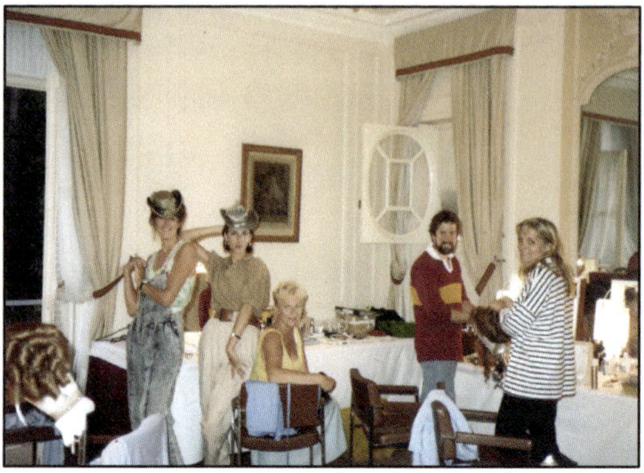

Dressing wigs for the next day

At the start of being scheduled onto any drama we receive the scripts, which have to be gone through with a fine-tooth comb to find out exactly what the make-up requirements will be. This could mean the ageing of artistes over many years, as I had when we did *Sophia and Constance* by Arnold Bennett. Some of the cast would start off as children and go on to old age, in which case they often cast three different people for the main characters so that the make-up doesn't have so much to do; but all the not-so-main characters in the story have a lot of work to be done with the continuous progress of ageing around the main artistes. This sort of story presents the most headaches for the make-up team, especially when they shoot the sequences out of story order.

For example, all the scenes for the whole story (covering 50 years) that take place in the kitchen will be performed in studio on the same day. This causes so much upset because it is going to mean delays and will keep the whole of the crew waiting for the make-up changes plus costume changes. As previous experiences prove, there is never enough time built into the film schedule for such events.

One of my biggest challenges came during the course of working on an adaptation of Arnold Bennett's book *The Sisters*, re-named *Sophia and Constance* for the TV production. I was never sure why titles were changed or who gave permission, but it was often the case when existing stories were used to make into films.

The cast was massive, partly because the changes in age were too great to perform with make-up. Hence, there were 3 Sophias and 3 Constances in every studio, as well as all the other cast members that could be aged successfully. The filming was to take place around the Potteries and in the Black Country Museum, as well as two weeks' filming in France; but first we were going to do all the studio scenes for the whole story, covering 50 years, and it was a worry as to how we could perform all the make-up ageing without causing some serious hold-ups. We were not over-done with help on busy days because there were two more major dramas on film and most of our girls had been allocated to them by the time I was setting up my team. Things were so bad that I had to talk one of our staff who had left to return just for the run of my filming. I then just had one Senior Assistant, Sue O'Neil, whose main occupation was looking after the three Sophias and supervising the two trainees who had only just arrived back from the make-up school and who I had taken on because there was no-one else to cover the show. It was all a bit 'nail-biting', but the two trainees were brilliant and took to the work like professionals; they were so good I couldn't believe my good fortune, because I was having to give them really difficult main artistes with wigs and beards and ageing to perform and they never complained or let me down.

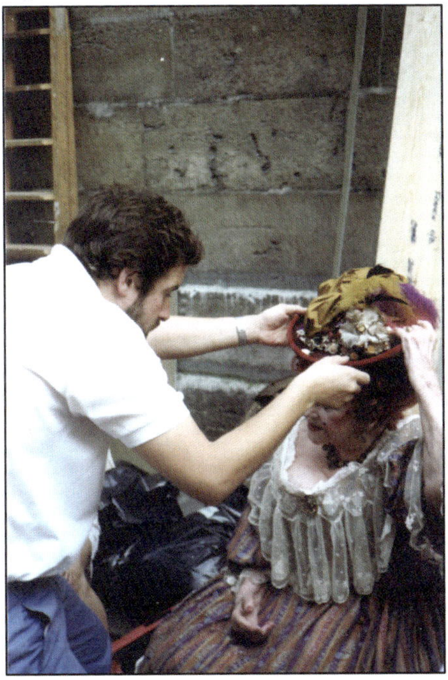

Final touches to Beryl Ried's hat

My thanks to Nicky and Val, and also Julia, the girl who got me out of trouble. There was also an old friend who I called upon from time to time: he had gone freelance years ago so that he could concentrate on doing prosthetics and special effects make-ups. I knew that one of the cast was going to be a handful and I knew that he had worked with her before, so I asked him to come with us just to look after her, and in the end Simon proved invaluable because he was able to help with a lot of the behind-the-scenes organising and getting us ready to move camp for the moves to the next locations when he wasn't on set with his artiste.

Something that isn't generally known is that a make-up artist must be with their actor at all times when they are on-camera in case there is a need for touching up. Fortunately, Simon's 'lady' didn't have many scenes in France and he was my willing slave, packing skips and cleaning and dressing wigs back at base.

On the set at the Palace of Versailles

So we got the show on the road and had some marvellous experiences. After the very heavy studio days it was a relief to be on such an exciting journey. We were going to Senlis first and then Rouen and on to Versailles and back to Paris. I had paid a flying visit with our production manager to check the make-up facilities that we would be using and had never been to any of those places before, so it was such a privilege to be taken to these fabulous places as part of my job. We had even been booked into the Trianon Palace in Versailles, which was as a special treat because we were all working so hard and would not be spending much time there to enjoy it; but when we arrived it was such a luxury to enter into such an historic hotel.

The next day was scheduled for 80 supporting artistes to be prepared for a scene in the Bois de Boulogne, so we were up half the night getting the make-up room ready and setting up the wigs ready for a quick start next morning. Thank heaven the weather was fine and it was the most awesome sight to see all our supporting artistes promenading around the spectacular gardens. At the end of the day, as another treat, we were taken back to the hotel in the horse-drawn landau. It really made all the work worthwhile.

The night shoot of the Guillotining

But our first location was Senlis, which was where Sophia – who had run away with her handsome debonair husband – went to watch the revolutionaries guillotining the aristocracy. This was an epic day of work to prepare 80 supporting artistes into the 'rough and ready citizens' of that period to be on set by evening, and thankfully only two main artistes, Sophia and Gerald. We started at about 11am working in the village hall where we had set up our work places the night before, after we had travelled from England, so we were not as fresh as we might have been; but the excitement got the adrenalin flowing and we were soon cracking along with much hilarity with our attempts to converse with the local French artistes. They were marvellous and threw themselves into this opportunity to practise their English, but even so the language barrier made heavy work of our day; there was so much that we wanted to transmit to them that didn't get through. Some of them were 'poutins', ladies of the night, and they loved the OTT make-up that we gave them.

Gerald as a young man

The weather was very hot and the only sustenance we had all day was water, so we were beginning to flag by the time we got them all on location and then we were there until the small hours of the morning. The best English then came out of the artistes, who by then were so tired that all they shouted for were 'Encore le Wet Wipes', so that they could remove some of their make-up and go home. We were truly exhausted, but we still had a long coach ride back to the hotel.

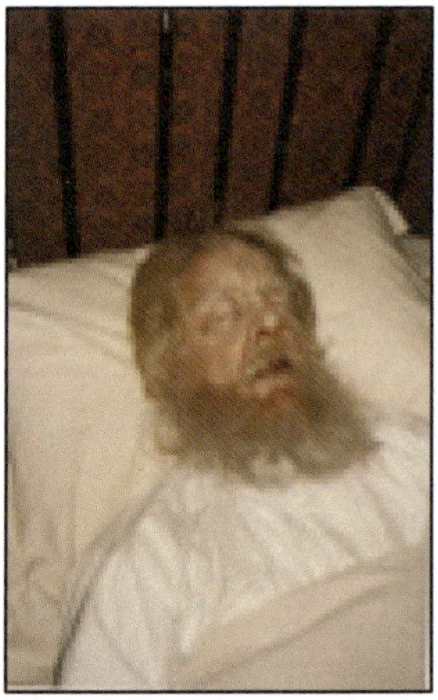

Gerald's death scene

Every day of the filming was as busy, with supporting artistes sometimes in very grand settings like the Bois de Boulogne at Versailles. We were spending every spare minute cleaning and re-dressing facial hair and wigs for the next day and there seemed a never-ending line of people waiting to be prepared and they all needed a considerable amount of work; but somehow we got through, even though there were only five of us.

When we returned to England we were pretty weary and we still had weeks of work to do up in Derbyshire and then on to the Black Country Museum for another two weeks. It was then that a bombshell fell. Early on in the preparations and setting up of the show, the director had talked to me about the eventual discovery by 'old Sophia' of the dead husband who had abandoned her in France, who by now had become a down-and-out tramp. He thought that they would use a very old extra as a cadaver that I could just mess up a bit and dirty down.

Dining room scene in Pebble Mill Studio

When he came to see me on our return he said he was concerned that this would not work and that they wanted there to be something recognisable about the dead Gerald. He wanted Sophia to see what he had sunk to. Could I make a nose or something to put on the face? What did I think? I was horrified and said no. My mind was in a whirl; I hadn't had any time to give this any thought. I had not expected there to be such a huge turn round; after all, it had been decided before we went to France. I had dismissed it from my mind. Thankfully, I got my wits together and suggested it would be better to use the real Gerald and I could make him old and grotty. I thought the director was going to explode with relief and I got the chance to pull out all the stops and did my finest transformation ever and loved every minute of it. They even gave me as much time as it took to prepare the finished 'body; a rare treat when, under most circumstances, everyone is twitching and demanding that they MUST have the artiste on set. We had had plenty of that going on during the studio when the ageing changes proved to be too long. To speed things up as much as possible, I had worked on the face and my assistant Nicky did the hands and poor Gerald just had to stay very still while we destroyed his face. It was a huge success; I even got a letter of thanks from the producer, John Harris. I still have it, but it isn't 'framed'.

As so often happens on big productions, there are some quite big names with very small parts or 'cameo roles'.

Beryl Reid was one such actress in *Sophia and Constance.* Playing the part of an old 'putin' (lady of the night), her storyline took place in France on location and in studio at Pebble Mill.

I had to go to London to meet her and discuss her make-up and wig, which I was using out of our stock as her part didn't justify the huge cost of having one made (around £500 in those days). I took several wigs for her to try in order to achieve the best fit. They were rehearsing her in an old church hall in Church Street, Kensington. I never did find out why they weren't at Acton, but maybe it was because Beryl lived too far away. Anyway, there were no facilities for me to use, not even a decent ladies' loo with a mirror. Since I had travelled up by train that morning, I had kept my kit to a minimum and so, as well as my necessary pins and combs, I only had a standard size hairdresser's back mirror with me.

This did not go down at all well as the lady didn't consider that she could see enough of the wig from every angle. All I can say is that I was left in no doubt that I had a very difficult actress on my hands and that was the last thing I needed on such a demanding production.

I don't think she liked the idea that she wasn't having a wig made especially for her and had expected priority treatment. I resolved the problem by 'giving her to Simon'. He had worked with her once before and knew how to handle the difficulties and completely charmed her. He would disappear into her dressing room with a bottle of red wine and an hour later they would appear looking absolutely fabulous as the ageing 'Madame of the night'.

Another of these 'small parts' went to another famous actress, playing the mother of Sophia and Constance. She did have a wig made for her at great expense, but seemed unaware of the fragility of the delicate hair lace front because as soon as her make-up girl settled it carefully on to her head she would lunge at the mirror and scrabble her finger about in the top of it, saying she didn't like it looking too set and it needed some air in it. This reduced my assistant to tears and I must say I wasn't far off it myself. It is such a precise work of art to settle a wig in the correct position and to have the artiste attack it in that way was very upsetting. The silly thing was that once the wig was in place a very large Mob Cap was to be placed over it and very little of the front of it would show, but we still had to virtually reset the wig after every performance in order to keep it from turning into a bird's nest. Hair lace wigs are a nightmare if they aren't treated with the greatest care and at £500 a time it pays to look after them.

The only other ongoing problem was the lovely Julian Fellowes. Still not really famous at this time in his career (or maybe he just liked filming abroad), he was with us in France as one of Sophia's admirers. His character had been given a small chin beard, which after several hours of being on camera simply would not stay on. We teased Nicky, who was looking after him, because we thought he was doing it just to get her to come and stick it back on. She was such a pretty girl and much in demand by everyone; but it seemed he had some allergy going on that made the glue not work; it really was an on-going nightmare and in the end I did feel really sorry for both of them, and he was so apologetic. Julian was another of those actors who has

Simon Callow as Mr Micawber

become so famous since those early days before he wrote *Gosford Park*. But I always remember that beard we worked our minor miracle on.

The rest of the filming went without any more last-minute panics and was a wonderful experience in so many different ways.

One of the worst of these last-minute shocks had happened to me when we did *David Copperfield*. Bald caps were one part of our prosthetics training at the BBC make-up school. They had never been anything that I had needed to make since that time. It is a very time-consuming procedure consisting of layer upon layer of special plastic on to a wig block, each layer having to dry before the next, with every layer receding at the edge so that it will disappear when placed on the skin. It is possible to buy them from professional prosthetics makers who only do that work, but on this occasion I had no warning in time to send for them. Simon Callow was cast as Mr Micawber, and he very kindly agreed to shave his head for the part; but when the contract for his scenes finished he had to quickly start letting his hair grow back. It had just started to look like quite a good covering when we had to re-shoot some of his scenes and then the axe fell on me. I was mortified when I realised that I had to now use my knowledge of bald caps! I told Simon of my plight and he laughed and, in that wonderful throaty voice, he said, "Well, it will be very good practice for you then, Maggie!" My heart sank and I had to work every evening after the end of the shoot making new bald caps for the next day. He was right: it was very good practice and I hoped it would never happen again.

Another example of an extreme age change came during our filming for *David Copperfield*. Once again we had three Davids to cover the different ages that he went through in the story and most of the rest of the cast were adults that we were able to age with the addition of make-up and greying wigs; but Ham was going to be played by just one actor, Owen Teale. Owen was a man of about 30 years at the time and was going to start off in his role as Ham as a 17-year-old for his first appearance in the story and then later on he would be in his 40s.Fortunately, Owen had a naturally boyish face, even at 30, and this made my life bearable in making a convincing attempt at a 17-year-old. After that the ageing was very straightforward as the addition of facial hair always has a considerable ageing effect as you can see from the pictures. I have included some of the other characters who appeared in this epic; another Period Drama that cost thousands of pounds and has only ever been broadcast once – in spite of the popularity of period drama.

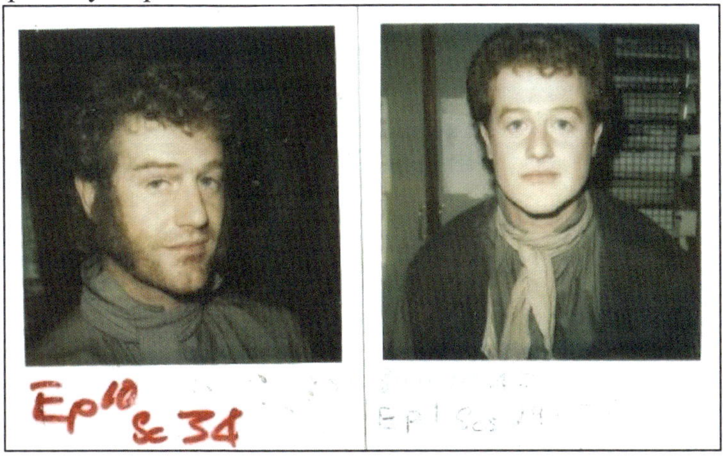

Owen Teel as old and young Ham

Another big Dickens production that brought its problems was *The Old Curiosity Shop*. We started shooting with Patrick Troughton on the Great Manchester Ship Canal for the scenes of Quip's Yard at night, another freezing cold time of year, and Patrick had a huge make-up and wig job to look the part, with blackened teeth and nails and general grime on all skin areas that were visible when the costume went on. The main character performance came from Patrick squatting down into a very strange deformed walk, which gave a brilliant look to this very eccentric character. We spent several nights doing these scenes and with the intense cold Patrick was getting exhausted from the awkward position he was adopting. Then we finished and returned to Birmingham to prepare for the studio scenes. A few days later we heard that Patrick was in hospital and would not be fit to continue his work as Quilp. The part had to be recast and we had to go back and shoot all these scenes again with Trevor Peacock. Trevor was a very good replacement and soon got into the character just as Patrick had. His costume and make-up took a lot of time in preparation, but once completed he would stay like that for the whole day. Apart from re-doing his blackened teeth after lunch, he needed very little maintenance.

However, this did cause a problem on one occasion. We were filming in Bridgnorth and Trevor had told me that he really wanted to go to Scotaid in his lunch break in the centre of the town to get his wife a silk blouse (they specialised in them at that time). He wanted to stay in his costume and wig to get a laugh out of the girls serving in the shop; and would I go with him. I can't say how the staff reacted, but it wasn't what Trevor had expected and they obviously thought he was a tramp. They were still not keen to serve him even after I had tried to explain the situation.

Another of the unexpected situations required of the Make-up Department.

John Savident as Creakle and Jeremy Brudenel as Steerforth

Another Fine Mess You Got Me In!

I can't actually remember when I was assigned to what was to be one of the most prestigious period productions that Pebble Mill had ever been commissioned to do. I had by now enough experience to cope with such a high profile drama, but I hadn't reckoned with the appalling problems that would arise from the choice of the Leading Lady who, for reasons that I never understood, was to be brought over from America. She had made her name in the film *Yanks* and someone in 'high places' decided she would be perfect for the part of the English lady who becomes so badly disfigured in a train crash that when she returns to her family in the guise of the 'Nanny to her own children' they don't recognise her.

The title was *East Lyn* and it was to be a big Christmas special feature film quality event. I realised that, with a cast of 58 main speaking famous artistes and a major work of art on this one character, I had better enlist the help of a very good prosthetics specialist, since I would have my work cut out dealing with the mechanics of getting the show on the road. I assigned one of my best make-up assistants to devote her entire time to the project and enlisted Aaron Sherman, the most highly skilled prosthetics man in the business, to create the very latest in foam pieces that would achieve the required effect without too much discomfort for the actress, as they would have to be applied and removed every day for several weeks.

I had all this in place by the time she was due to appear for the tests and had booked a make-up room at London TV Centre for us to meet and have a chance for Aaron to show my assistant how to achieve the best results with the featherlight foam pieces that he had made. The actress was so lucky that he had been able to make them without her having to have a 'face-cast' in plaster of paris, which is a really horrible experience for anyone.

The pieces he made were the very latest technique in prosthetics and were going to cost a fortune because of the need to use them for so many of the scenes that she was in. Sam and I were really looking forward to the opportunity of having this 'master class' with an expert.

I think someone had mentioned vaguely that the actress would be bringing her own small child who would have a very small part in the story, but it didn't occur to me that she would be bringing it to the make-up test. Nor had the producer or director thought to mention to me that her husband was one of the famous American film WESTMORE family and was also a make-up man. So, when they all pushed a baby- buggy into the very small make-up room at TV Centre, I was speechless. I imagined when she introduced her husband he was going to go off with the child while we got on with the test; still unaware that he was a major film make-up man. Even though the director and producer had brought them in to the room, they did not have the good manners to mention it. I WAS COMPLETELY IN THE DARK.

I felt so embarrassed for poor Aaron trying to do his work with this 'circus' going on around him and the father and child making no move to leave.

The pieces were a work of art and Sam and I were thrilled with the chance to watch him at work; but it was quite obvious from 'madam's' face that she was displeased and very quickly, before Aaron could properly complete his work, she was getting up to leave and pulling the pieces off, regardless of the quality of the work or the consideration of the preparation that had gone into the work. She and her family SWEPT out of the room. Aaron, Sam and I were left with our jaws on the floor, hardly able to believe what we had just witnessed. I sent Sam home and proceeded up to the production office to try and explain the situation to the producer, not knowing how to explain just what had gone on. I had never before been in such an embarrassing position in my whole career.

The outcome of all this bad behaviour was that the star had no intention of having anyone but her husband to do her make-up and the producer and his sidekick director David

Green had known this all along, but hadn't the manners to let me in on the secret. They just wanted to keep her happy at ALL costs, regardless of what we were trying to do. The producer insisted that I must allow Mr. Westmore to do a make-up test to show how it should be done and I felt powerless to refuse.

I was allowed to see the result of the test from the studio gallery, where we could view it on a monitor. The result was an outrageous farce. The 'injury' he did was just like a small scar on her cheek, no bigger than a small sticking plaster. We were also told that she didn't like my assistant (who had not even spoken to her on the day of our test) and would only have her husband to do her make-up.

I think I had a brainstorm. I said I would not have my name attached to such a 5th-rate excuse for an injury, since the whole story hinged around the fact that her injuries were so disfiguring that her family couldn't recognise her. How could it possibly be used? I went to my union and, to cut a long story short, it was stopped. Since we are not allowed to work in America without a Green Card, he had no right to work here. The whole production went on to be a nightmare and all the crew had a public apology broadcast on Milfax and the 'Terrible Two' were told they would never work for the BBC again.

There was one very funny story to come out of the rather stressful days.

We were working at the beautiful mansion house that was being featured as the family home and Rodney Bewes (of *The Likely Lads*) was playing the part of the owner. We were all outside shooting some scenes of a coach arriving. Suddenly, we heard the sound of alarm bells ringing and up the drive came a fire engine.

Unbeknown to us, Rodney, who was inside the house waiting until he was needed for his scenes, had gone into the lounge to sit down and wait, and, as it was rather chilly in the room, he had put a match to the fire laid in the grate and before he knew what was happening the chimney was on fire.

I know we will always remember him for 'light' entertainment, but that was NOT what he was expecting!

We all collapsed laughing, but he was truly shocked at the trouble he had caused.

Just one more story in a lighter vein to come out of this was a visit to the hairdresser with Tim Woodward (son of Edward). His hair at this time was quite an unruly mop and, with the style of the character being a dashing military look, I decided that a 'very soft' perm would make it much more manageable. We didn't have time to be setting men's hair every day and so I made an appointment with a hairdresser that I used regularly because they were reliable and didn't mind doing exactly what was required for the character.

I had only met Tim briefly once before and found him good natured and easy to discuss the needs of his character. He seemed quite happy to go along with the perm.

When the perm was finished the hairdresser did a 'blow-dry' so that he could see the benefit of the perm. He seemed quite content and off he went and I returned to Birmingham. The next day I received a phone call – it was Tim, telling me that he was going to 'scalp' me. Apparently, when he left the shop he went home – on his motorbike – and when he arrived to where he was meeting his friends, he took his helmet off and they all started laughing. Because he had sweated in the helmet, it had turned his 'soft perm' into bubbly curls all over his head.

What could I say? I had no idea that he even had a motorbike. Fortunately for me, he had a good sense of humour and he let me off the scalping.

A Challenge Of A Different Kind

One of the great charms of the job was the extreme variation in the content of the productions. I have talked a lot about the period dramas and the heavy working hours involved with preparation and maintenance of the wigs and hairpieces, so to go on to a production like *Boys from the Black Stuff* is like chalk and cheese and I couldn't say which would be a favourite. It was the opportunity to do such different things in very different places that kept the adrenalin flowing. I hadn't before and never did again work on a film quite like *The Black Stuff*. We moved into the Adelphi in Liverpool, lock stock and barrel, for a 6-month stint that had the most exciting buzz about it. We set up our delegated make-up rooms and unpacked our own clothes. It was the most extreme luxury that I had ever stayed in. The bathrooms had baths 4-feet deep in the middle of the marble-clad room. The only trouble was, it took an hour to fill. Down in the basement was a beautiful swimming pool that we made good use of after work. Some of the public rooms were like something in a royal palace. Sadly, it was all a bit faded and years later, when they made a film about it, I think it was nearly at the end of its heyday.

Bernard Hill as Yosser

Once again our trusted coach driver would be our sanctuary every day on every location. Little did we know how important that would be in Liverpool at that time. We always had so many valuable work items with us all the time and some of the locations were in very run-down parts of the city and it hadn't been long since the Toxteth riots.

Most of the cast for the first of the five stories were in Liverpool by now and started to come for discussions with the director and me as to what was needed for their storyline. As they were mostly portraying hard times, my job was only going to be roughing them up and de-smartening them. This was my one and only time of working with the fabulous Julie Walters. She was so professional about looking really drab with almost no make-up, but her sense of fun shone through her really harrowing character in the story and for the short time we had with her in the make-up room she had us in fits of laughter. She deserves every accolade in the book.

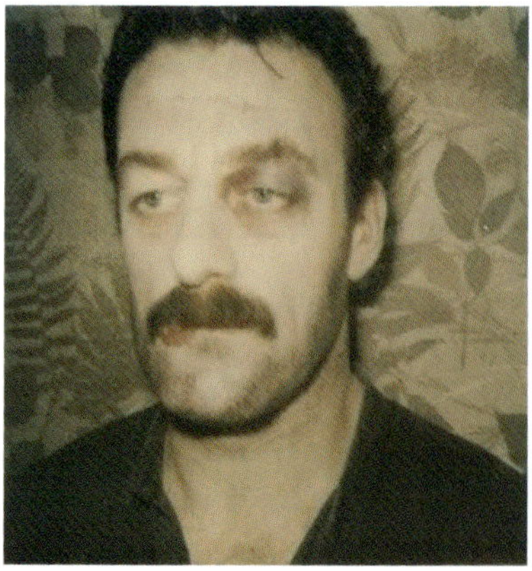

The five episodes were complete stories about the five characters. The main storyline was 'Yosser's Story' and Bernard Hill had to appear as the character that he had established on a previously shot pilot film just called *The Black Stuff*, so I had no say in any of their make-up. I was told that Bernard no longer had the moustache that he had grown for the part, but I had several made that we could use in case he had not had time to grow his own. When he eventually came up to Liverpool to start his episode, he came to see me only the day before the shoot. I was shocked to see that his hair was a mousy brown, not nearly dark enough for the Yosser look. Time was running out and I had to resort to something unheard of, and that was to try to tint his hair myself. I was used to using Nice'N'Easy on my own mousy locks, but I have never applied a dark colour. That was something we always had done professionally at a hairdresser in London. Bernard agreed that we would have to try, so I applied the colour. I knew enough to be very careful around the hairline and had smeared his skin with Vaseline to protect it, but, in spite of this, when the colour developed there were some areas that were going dark purple before my eyes. I could have cried, but could do nothing to stop it. When the time was up and we washed off the dye we had to go to work on the purple patches with Vim, which is a rather powerful sink bleach. Bernard was so patient and didn't make any fuss at all; just as well, as we were about to embark on several weeks of some of the most challenging scenes requiring the most ongoing sequences of injuries on anyone I had ever worked with.

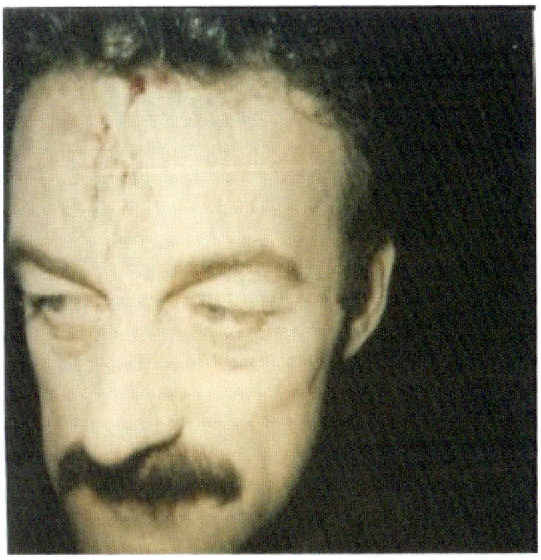

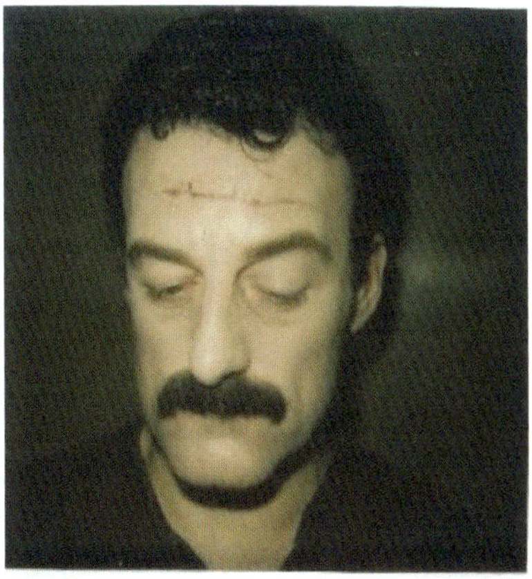

Yosser's story was full of head banging and brutal beatings and so we spent many happy hours creating his layer upon layer of injuries throughout his filming.

Most of the rest of the cast were just natural as they had appeared in the pilot and I was very relieved to see that Michael Angelis still had his marvellous mop of curls. Some of the stories were electrifying and the scenes with Michael and Julie were heartbreakingly realistic. It was so close to the real-life stories that were all around in Liverpool at that time. There was so much hardship and the Toxteth riots had only happened the previous year.

This all took place before the reinventing of the old dock area and some of the scenes we shot there for 'George's' story were very atmospheric. I could feel the ghosts in the ether as Michael pushed Peter Kerrigan (playing George) in his wheelchair on his last journey before he was about to die. It was very moving. The docks were all closed or closing and Liverpool was really on the way down. When it was announced that they were going to turn them into gardens it was hard to imagine how that could possibly help the huge numbers of people who couldn't get work, but somehow the spirit of Liverpudlians can never be squashed for long and the making of the gardens was just the start of the long climb back up the ladder. I have most of the stories of the 'Boys' on tape and when I watched them to refresh my memory I wondered why they have never been shown again. The quality of the acting and storylines is so good. I think it would show a few people how far this city has risen from the ashes of the early 80s.

All of this may sound such an exciting, fulfilling and glamorous life. I have been fortunate in working in the industry for the most fruitful years of its development. My years at the BBC were certainly the happiest of my life. Not because of excitement and glamour, but more because it was like being part of a big family who worked, played and cried together. Until the axe fell in 1987 and the accountants moved in, it was impossible to imagine life outside the embrace of such security.

People loved their work and the goodwill flowed. Overtime was paid, but all departments would always work beyond the call of duty and the quality of programme choice at Pebble Mill in those years extended far beyond the lunch-time programme. Being a drama region meant that we hosted lots of London productions: as well as having our own Drama Department we worked a 7-day week studio because it was cheaper to bring the drama out of London and into Birmingham at that time. Our scenes crew would be on all-night breakdown of sets that were finished and build-ups for the next production. The whole building buzzed with activity and the stimulation to be in such surroundings was invigorating, in spite of the tremendous pressures of the long unsociable hours, long periods spent away from home, never having time off when friends were having Bank Holidays or birthday parties; work came first, regardless of disappointments, and we were all happy to be in our jobs.

I always felt that the powers that were in London at that time just couldn't ever give Pebble Mill Birmingham the credit that was due for the years of quality productions that were of the highest standards expected by the BBC.

The beginning of the end was caused by the discovery that the Manager of all the Scenic Services was creaming off thousands of pounds and had been for a number of years. For instance, it was discovered that on the farm that he owned in Scotland he had a BBC generator to supply the electricity. This was just the tip of the iceberg and the exposé started when he arranged for a set of Harem and Sultan's clothes to be made by the Costume Department for him to wear along with selected members of staff as his "Harem Girls" to go to an Arrivals Party that was being held by a local newspaper, the idea being "who could arrive in the most outrageous fancy dress". Then, of course, there were pictures of it all in the evening newspaper. Bad move. Instant dismissal.

After that the accountants moved in and our lives were run by faceless people who had no understanding of the work that we did. The Goodwill, Loyalty, Talent, Expertise, suddenly counted for nothing. Only the columns of figures and balancing the books and cutting budgets were what the new regime wanted. We even had our bags searched when we left the building. Everyone felt under suspicion and nothing was ever the same again.

It started the demise of Pebble Mill and from then on there was the feeling that the powers that be in London were looking for a reason to shut the place down.

I think it was the most wicked act that has ever happened. Pebble Mill was a state-of-the-art, purpose-built superb Studio and Sound Recording Studio and had only been opened by HRH Princess Anne in 1971, and by 1990 they started looking for people to take early retirement or voluntary redundancy, and now in 2007 it is just a pile of rubble. Thanks to the faceless 'powers'.

I should write some more about the bitterness that was felt at the time but, as I was so long gone, I didn't really have any first-hand gossip. It is just my own sadness that such a wonderful place should end with so little respect.

After the shaming and subsequent dismissal of one of the 'top brass' at Pebble Mill, everyone was under a microscope. Every departmental head was scrutinised for every penny spent.

There was also at this time a huge investigation going on into the London Costume Department, but we were usually too busy to take much notice. However, this was the beginning of the end of the BBC as we knew it. The accountants took over and very soon people were going to be offered redundancies or early retirement.

Our Head of Department Gwen was retiring and I had reached a point where I should be applying to become Head of Department, along with a couple of other members of staff who were also in the running for it. I couldn't imagine anything worse than becoming a pen-pusher and having to deal with 'The Management' on a daily basis. Also, in a climate of people's jobs being axed and forced redundancies, early retirement appeared my best option, or so it seemed at the time.

Back To Square 1

So, in 1990 I flew the nest, and what a nest it was. I had never been in a position of finding my own work and, as a freelance make-up artist, this was paramount to success. We had always used freelances at Pebble Mill because we were such a small department and our office had lists of qualified girls who came and went and always gave the impression that the grass was very much greener in their world, with a chance to pick and choose their own jobs and have lots of time off in between. Also, the rates of pay sounded fantastic. They were able to claim travel expenses, half a day (4 hours) travel pay, plus hotel accommodation for overnight stays and then another 4 hours to travel home, on top of a high hourly rate of pay.

So I set about getting my printing done – headed notepaper, business cards, CV, etc. – and started blasting them off to every television company in the land. The travel part of the work didn't seem too much of a problem since I had always done so much filming, which always involved travel and as BBC staff we were paid travel expenses and whatever lodgings we stayed in by way of a lump sum that we collected from the cash office prior to going on location; we also had hire cars to use.

A Step Down Or 2!

It was a complete bombshell when the first good offer of work came in. I was to do *Soldier Soldier* (the very first one in the series), on the condition that I would accept what was called a buy-out. This was an agreement to accept a monthly sum of money – end of. No overtime, no travel expenses, no hotels paid for. I felt in my bones I should not turn this down as it was to be nine months' work and would get me used to going it alone. What I didn't immediately realise was that I would only be an Assistant Make-up Artist. So I was back to starting all over again.

Fortunately, the make-up designer was a girl I knew from Central Television, Birmingham, and she treated all of us like equals. So we were a very happy bunch and, in spite of the fall in my status, I thoroughly enjoyed my nine months. Luckily, a lot of the locations were very close to where I lived and the most travelling I had to do was only to the army barracks at Lichfield.

Our main work to start with was extreme short back and sides for practically everyone. Robson had a No. 2 clippers all over, which I had fortunately practised on my son; it is not something that is very common to have to do, but I think it was also becoming a fashion round about then. 'The Boys' were really up for it and soon got into military behaviour after some gruelling training. Robson and Jerome immediately formed a strong friendship and were often found to be suffering from too much 'enjoyment' the next morning. We had bought ourselves a toaster for the make-up caravan, which already had a coffee maker, so we were very popular on their early morning calls to revive them with black coffee and toast. It was too cold to go and stand in a queue for breakfast and took up too much of our time, so our toaster was the best buy ever.

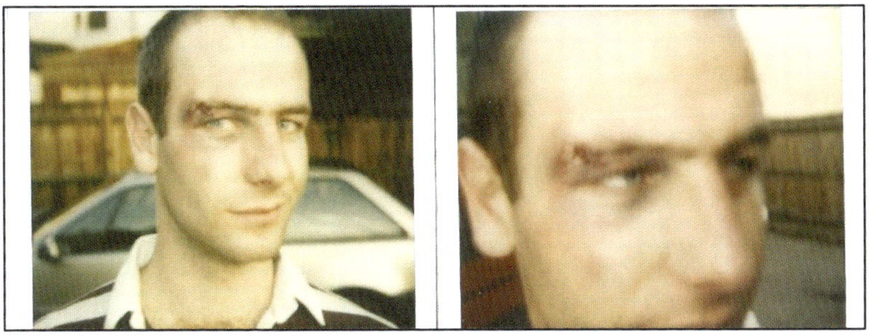

Giving Robson Green a black eye in Soldier Soldier

Needless to say, the make-up requirements were mostly camouflage for the soldiers and on the days that we had to do it we were nearly as messed up as them. When there are about 40 soldiers lined up to have 'face painting' it is too time consuming, so we devised a solution by getting the supporting cast to do each other and pass the tin along.

The army wives were our only proper make-ups and a very light relief from all the clipping and messing up on the lads. I also had a nice injury to do on Robson, which made some more interest for those scenes. It can be very tedious day after day in very cold weather to just have to stand around with hardly any maintenance to do on the artistes. It makes the time go very slowly. Even Holly Aird, our lone female soldier, didn't really need much more than her hair tied back.

So it all got finished and we all went our separate ways. Some of the crew were Central Television staff and one day during filming someone came out on location from their office to tell them that Central Studios Birmingham was being closed down. I felt so sorry for them. What a disgusting way to notify staff who had worked there for probably more than 20 years that they no longer had a job.

It was a body blow to me too as I had hoped to get more work from them as it was so close to home. They did continue for a bit longer, but I didn't do much there after that. I started getting a lot of work from Central Nottingham and then I realised what a cushy time I had enjoyed at Pebble Mill. Having to drive for an hour or more in heavy traffic every time I went there just made the job so much harder and by now they had done away with all the perks of the job as it had been, so there were no 4-hour travel and overnight payments, not even petrol payments. Hey ho! It soon becomes the norm and I soon settled into the new life and had a lot of very happy times at Nottingham. It was much more like my early days at ATV Aston. All light entertainment in studio and one of my maddest encounters yet: Freddy Starr.

I won't say too much, but it was like a roller-coaster. I don't think Freddy himself knows just what he is going to do next. He is the nicest, most unpredictable person and just wants to make everyone around him laugh all the time. It was like being drunk on laughter and he just never stopped. Happy days.

Bobby Davro was another favourite. I did a whole series with him and was amazed at his superb talent for impersonations. I was in my element, as my most favourite work is doing transformations, and he was a joy to work with. He did Michael Winner, Eamon Holmes and Bob Hoskins, who was the actor in *Roger Rabbit*, and Maureen Lipman as Aunty BT, and many more that I can't remember; but it was so rewarding to put in so much effort for such a great result.

I also had the good fortune to do Honor Blackman's make-up for the sitcom that was a regular in studio at Central Nottingham in those days. *The Upper Hand* was about a male housekeeper played by Joe McGann. She has to be the most elegant, beautiful actress that it has been my privilege to do and truly did not have loads of make-up. She just has beautiful skin and bone structure that needs so little to add to her looks. The only other lady I worked with similar to this was Selina Scott on *The Clothes Show*; she too had that marvellous natural beauty.

I was really never out of work for long, but there was always that sinking feeling at the end of every job as to how long it would be before something else came along. I did do quite a lot for Granada on the *Sherlock Holmes Mysteries*, but I hated the journey on the M6. Even that long ago it was a nightmare of uncertainty as to how long any journey would take, so I always had to travel the day before and stay in a grotty pub near to the studios as most of the work was done in the make-up room before going out to locations around Manchester. Often these would only be one or two days and then there would be the horrid journey back at the end of an extremely tiring day. I was getting too old to want many of these jobs.

The Beginning of the End – Peak Practice

Moving on to *Peak Practice* probably gave me my worst working experience to date.

I had done a couple of days from time to time when they had crowd scenes. Just to take the occasional day's work is vital at times; as a freelance we never know when a long run will be offered, that is a 1- to 6-month shoot as a full-time member of the team. Usually only two or three people are required to cover the work on a modern drama shot on location. This is partly because every-day make-up can be managed more quickly than a period production and partly because the budget available on such things as *Peak Practice* do not allow for anything except the minimum amount of attention to artistes. There is a passage in this book explaining the formal procedures of a make-up artist's involvement with the pre-shoot necessities of the job. On *Peak Practice* none of these requirements are observed. They treated the Make-up Designer like a nonentity, but this is the general attitude that pervades the whole thing. Script management is non-existent; even the leading actors sometimes only get a new episode script the day before, but they are expected to go on set and perform their part faultlessly. Then there are the late amendments to scripts that may be delivered to them at any time, late at night or first thing in the morning, when they are sitting in the make-up chair. This can often mean that the lines already learned for the day's work ahead all have to be re-learned with the new additions or deletions, making a nonsense of the work they have put in previously. Is it surprising when actors decide they won't do another series of such a shambolic nature? It can only be said that *Peak Practice* III only came to the viewers because of the outstanding professionalism of the two leading actors and the loyalty and support of the whole crew who every day worked beyond the call of duty and also over their scheduled hours for no thanks or pay by the worst production team it has been my experience to encounter. The producer never appeared on set; the usual BBC producer is there most days to see that things run smoothly and that unnecessary wastage of resources can be avoided by their presence. Who will ever know what a highly paid lady was doing, but it sure as hell was not in her contract. On the rare occasions that she did turn up (just in time for a free lunch), she seemed only able to have the most trivial conversations about her dog or baby or what her star sign said. We all found this very insulting since we had been up at work since 6.30am in often very cold and wet conditions and would continue long after her departure until around 8.00pm that night.

These trials and tribulations were thankfully unknown to me when I received a phone call from the Designer on the shoot asking me to join the team for a 3-month period from January to April 1994. I was dumbfounded. I would love to do the job, but I would not return from my Christmas in America until 19th January. Would that be too late? It was explained to me that I was only needed to do Amanda Burton's make-up and that she would cover for me until I returned. Brilliant.

The day came and back came the butterflies. Why on earth had they wanted me? What could I do that was so special? The answers soon came when I started to work with Amanda. She had been exposed to such awful weather conditions over a prolonged period and her skin was so scalded by windburn and even her ears had chilblains on the edges and unfortunately her previous make-up artist had to leave due to her inability to cope with prevailing conditions and affairs of the heart!

I will say no more, except that there followed one of the happiest partnerships in my working life and at the end of the three months Amanda invited me to do the next series. The current producer was leaving and new people would take over, but if she had asked for me it would be fairly safe to know I would be working again from August 1994 to March 1995, an 8-month run – wonderful.

I should have seen the red light and run myself. Eight months of getting up at 5.30am and working until 8.30pm. Would the old bones stand such a long stint in that cold weather in the Peak District?

Well they did and we all got through, but it wasn't much fun. I promised myself then that I would not take on any more work for such a long period of time.

As I have explained earlier, the work was made so much harder by the new production team being so shambolic. Those of us with years of experience could not believe that such a high-profile production with such large viewing figures could be put into the hands of such incompetent managers. The truth of the matter is that most television companies now are being run by accountants and puppets that have no knowledge of the work at the grass roots of the industry and very little interest in human relations; to understand a workforce that functions on goodwill and pulling together in every type of adverse situation. Racing through dark and icy roads at 6am to be sure not to be late with giant granite quarry lorries looming round every bend in the road so fast and big it seemed impossible that they would not crush you. In the half-awake state at that time in the depths of winter it sometimes seemed that death would be preferable to continuing. These are not things that accountants could begin to understand. Their minds are only capable of looking into columns of figures to see if they are making a profit for the shareholders and a big fat bonus for themselves. So, if the front-line cannon fodder is falling like flies, just replace them; there are plenty more queuing up to do the job.

While, for technical reasons, the director has to go for take after take there is more waiting around while the lighting man changes all the light positions. During this time the main artistes will return to their caravans and stand-ins will hold their positions for the lighting change. Before every take the make-up artist will check the face, usually powder a little and add lipstick, but that is usually the most attention the actual make-up gets all day, unless there is kissing or crying in the storyline.

Often the shoot will have to wait if an injury takes place during the dialogue, but then they usually have some lighting changes to make; once these are complete they start hassling the make-up artist to hurry up with her work on the injury. This is often very annoying as some injury make-up is very complicated and needs time for the different stages to settle and dry. My worst experience was on *Peak Practice*.

A first-on-set artiste with all of his scenes that day came into the make-up caravan late because he had cut his head on a glass shelf over his wash basin in the hotel. I had to hold ice cubes on to try to stop the bleeding, then build up a new forehead. First, I put butterfly strips, followed by new skin, followed by spirit sealer, then spirit gum, then the special wax used for making false noses to cover the whole area and make it blend with his own forehead, then more sealer. A normal make-up call for a man would be 20 minutes. This took close on 2 hours! Once again I was given time to do the job, but there was still a lot of pressure to get him out on location as he had to return to London after his scenes because of another acting commitment.

The Very End

Another low-profile but crucial member of any period drama is the Props Buyer, the unsung hero of the Design Department. The Designers at Pebble Mill were mostly very young men with outstanding talent for set design. The opportunities that presented themselves at that time in television were like manna from heaven. Our managers were getting more and more prestigious drama productions because the powers-that-be considered it was cheaper to use the facilities at Pebble Mill than Television Centre, London, and so everyone's talents were given the best programmes on which to flex their muscles, with some outstanding results. But behind the scenes there was an area of work that relied on some expert knowledge; that spot was filled by props buyers. They knew all the London hire companies and would take the lists of furniture and *objets d'art* required by the Designer to create exactly the correct look for the period. Tom Beech was one of the most knowledgeable buyers and he was with us for *All Creatures Great and Small.* Although he would occasionally come on location, his work was mostly in London, shopping for the sets in studio. Every teaspoon and toilet roll had to be exactly right and Tom was a vital part of the end product.

The next unsung members of any crew are the scenic builders who often work through the night to assemble all the huge scenic flats, which are the walls of the rooms in studio. I would compare their jobs to moving house every day and we all know how stressful that can be. Every picture and footstool has to be in place by the start of the shoot. When we filmed parts of *Sophia and Constance* at the Black Country Museum, the scene crew built a whole new street in the centre of the main town. It was only if you looked behind the shop fronts that you could see the scaffold poles holding it together. These shops were where the family lived and worked, but the scenes inside were at Pebble Mill studios.

So every department is just as important to the production, but unfortunately they don't always get the recognition on the credits that roll at the end of the film. There are so many more behind the scenes crew that never get their name in lights.

My last working days were spent in Bristol on *Casualty*. One hour on the M5 at

5.30am seemed almost enjoyable after the M6.

One of the girls who had often come to Pebble Mill as a freelance and worked on some of my productions rang me to say that she was now doing a lot of work on *Casualty* and would I like to come and help her. It was usually only the occasional day to start with, but as time went by I was offered more and more days and she was kind enough to put me up at her home. They were very happy days, with lots of injuries to do. The set-up is really just the same as a studio, except the medical sets are permanent and there are some very expensive state-of-the-art pieces of equipment and they are just built inside what would be described as industrial warehouse units. Then the exterior shots of the ambulances are on the other side of town, outside one of the colleges where the emergencies arrive and go in through the doors which the scenic department dress with the usual A&E logos.

During my later days doing this I started to get a lot of pain in one of my hips and became less and less able to do the job; with so much equipment to carry around it just wasn't practical, but it was a really nice end to a brilliantly happy career.

A Resume

I'm sorry if I have 'banged on' about BBC Pebble Mill, but I have felt for a long time that it was so undervalued.

I never recovered from the shock of seeing the pile of rubble in Pebble Mill Road. I still feel angry all these years later.

The whole place was such a centre of excellence. I weep for all the talent that was thrown on the scrapheap.

My story is just a tiny part of what was done there. As well as the productions I have mentioned, there were hundreds more going on at the same time and many more that I did work on that would probably make another book.

So now they are spending your money on a BRAND NEW STATE OF THE ART CENTRE AT SALFORD and I have become A GRUMPY OLD LADY!

Happy Days…

Finally my apologies for the very poor quality of some of the pictures throughout the book, but they are VERY OLD and most of them are Polaroid's taken for continuity of hair and make-up, not for pretty pictures.

Printed in the United States
1515LVUK00001B

9780755204533